I0813531

KEN CASTOR

The Bible Reading Plan Devotional

for Men

365 DAILY MEDITATIONS

BroadStreet
PUBLISHING

BroadStreet Publishing Group, LLC.
Savage, Minnesota, USA
Broadstreetpublishing.com

The Bible Reading Plan Devotional for Men

9781424571543
9781424571550 (eBook)

Devotional entries composed by Ken Castor.

Typesetting and design by Garborg Design Works | garborgdesign.com
Editorial services by Michelle Winger | literallyprecise.com and Natasha Marcellus.

Printed in China.

26 27 28 29 30 31 32 7 6 5 4 3 2 1

"Heaven and earth will pass away,
but my words will never pass away."

MATTHEW 24:35 CSB

Introduction

Do you long for a deeper connection with God and a greater understanding of his Word? *The Bible Reading Plan Devotional for Men* is designed to guide you through the entire Bible in one year.

Each entry includes carefully selected passages of Scripture, insightful meditations that bring biblical truths to life, and heartfelt prayers to help draw you closer to God and seek his wisdom in all areas of your life. Whether you're new to Bible reading or have been studying for years, this devotional will equip you to stay consistent, deepen your faith, and discover the transformative power of God's Word.

Open these pages and experience the value of walking through the Bible one day at a time. Let this year be the year you grow in faith, wisdom, and intimacy with your Creator.

January

Your word is a lamp for my feet
and a light on my path.

Psalm 119:105 csb

Scripture Reading: Genesis 1-3

God Speaks

In the beginning, God created the heavens and the earth. The earth was without form and void, and darkness was over the face of the deep. And the Spirit of God was hovering over the face of the waters. And God said, "Let there be light," and there was light.

GENESIS 1:1-3 ESV

After God finished creating this marvelous world, Scripture says that he looked it over and declared it to be very good. His Creation reflected his own glory and completeness. It was not lacking anything. It was pure, strong, and built with integrity. By his Word he created light, separated water and land, and filled the planet with living things. All he had to do was speak.

God's Word is essential to life. His good plans demand a posture of listening for his voice. His Spirit moves over each of us and is ready to guide us. His Word is ready to transform our hearts, shape our thoughts, and give purpose to all our endeavors. As a new year begins, let's incline our ears to hear what God is speaking over our goals and routines.

Dear Lord, you simply spoke and everything came into existence. Please speak into my life today. Create in me actions that will bring glory to your holy name.

Scripture Reading: Genesis 4-6

Standing Strong

This is the account of Noah and his family. Noah was a righteous man, blameless among the people of his time, and he walked faithfully with God.

GENESIS 6:9 NIV

God's initial declaration of goodness shifted when he saw the wickedness that had flourished. He observed how people had strayed from him, and he was grieved. The scene unfolding within his creation deeply troubled his heart.

Noah was different from the rest of the men on earth. He did not drown in the overwhelming flood of his culture. Instead, Noah found favor in the eyes of the Lord. He was like a beacon of light cutting through the fog. When God looked at Noah, he saw a man who stood in contrast to the evil actions of those around him. God saw a man whose heart aligned with righteousness and faithfulness. God saw a man who could be part of his daring plan of salvation for a broken world.

God, give me the courage today to stand strong as one who is faithful to you. May my thoughts and actions be righteous and pleasing to you.

Scripture Reading: Genesis 7-9

Trusting God

Two by two they came into the boat, representing every living thing that breathes. A male and female of each kind entered, just as God had commanded Noah. Then the Lord closed the door behind them.

Genesis 7:15-16 NLT

When God shut the door behind them, do you think Noah may have had a moment of panic? Everything he had known was outside that door, yet his new calling awaited inside, shut off from what was familiar. Scripture tells us that despite the difficulties of the tasks ahead, Noah was faithful. He followed God's instructions exactly as he gave them. Noah's devotion to God changed the trajectory of not just his life but the entirety of human existence.

Like Noah, we can be unwavering in our commitment to God's plans. We can stick to the journey even if we don't fully foresee the outcome. We can remain focused on our mission even if doors are shut behind us. Staying true to God's call might seem foolish to others, but it is a worthy pursuit. Our faithfulness will surely impact more than just ourselves.

Heavenly Father, empower me to act with integrity in everything I do. Give me grace to be faithful to the call you have placed on my life.

Scripture Reading: Genesis 10-12

Blessed through You

"I will bless those who bless you,
and whoever curses you I will curse;
and all peoples on earth
will be blessed through you."

Genesis 12:3 NIV

God doesn't give up on sinful, broken people. When Adam and Eve brought the consequence of sin to the world, God brought a sacrifice to cover their naked shame. When people embraced evil, God provided a plan to preserve life on earth through the righteousness of Noah. When society's leaders blasphemed God and built a tower exulting their own glory, God scattered them and launched a plan to bless all of humanity through the faithfulness of one man.

Every person God uses to execute his plans is part of a much bigger picture. Yes, God blessed Abram's faithfulness with success and leadership, but Abram's impact went beyond his lifetime. He created a legacy of obedience and righteousness. God blessed Abram's day-to-day life, and he equipped him with a faith that would become a blessing to all generations.

Lord, shape the work of my hands and the focus of my heart. Help me see the long-term impact of my decisions.

Scripture Reading: Genesis 13-15

Believing God

"Look up at the sky and count the stars—if indeed you can count them.... So shall your offspring be." Abram believed the LORD, and he credited it to him as righteousness.

GENESIS 15:5-6 NIV

God declared in a vision that Abram would have descendants as numerous as the stars in the sky. However, there was a major obstacle to that promise being realized. Abram and his wife were unable to have children. The Lord's promise seemed far-fetched and astonishing. Despite the impossible circumstances, Abram trusted what God said. He decided that God's promises were more powerful than his problems.

God's promises rarely come with a step-by-step manual. He doesn't typically give us a detailed explanation of how his plans will come to pass. His promises require faith. They often require us to move one step at a time, believing that he will weave the details together perfectly. It's not our responsibility to make sure everything fits together; it's our responsibility to keep our eyes on him and move forward bit by bit.

God, guide my steps and strengthen my faith. Help me follow you even when it doesn't make sense to me.

Scripture Reading: Genesis 16-18

Binding Agreement

When Abram was ninety-nine years old the LORD appeared to Abram and said to him, "I am God Almighty; walk before me, and be blameless, that I may make my covenant between me and you, and may multiply you greatly."

GENESIS 17:1-2 ESV

A covenant is a mutual promise or agreement. It requires a deliberate level of commitment that binds each partner to one another. From the moment of agreement onward, those who enter a covenant relationship are linked together. Understanding the seriousness of a covenant helps us understand God's covenant with Abram. God bound himself to a plan of salvation and in so doing demonstrated his love for all humankind.

When we chose to follow Jesus, we entered into God's covenant. We made a commitment to him, and we promised to be faithful. Like Abram, God asks us to believe in his promises and walk according to his ways. He asks us to trust in him so that we might have eternal life. God is holding up his end of the agreement. Would he say that we are holding up ours?

Lord, I am humbled that you would invite me into an eternal covenant with you. May I be found blameless through the work of Jesus Christ.

Scripture Reading: Genesis 19-21

Ideal Place

Abraham went early in the morning to the place where he had stood before the LORD.

GENESIS 19:27 ESV

Abraham had a place where he met with God. Abraham stood before the Lord amid sin and destruction. In a culture crippled by sin and on the brink of imploding, Abraham petitioned God to save his family. His response to the chaos around him was to meet with God. He took time to process his thoughts and experiences with the only one who could see it all clearly.

God is our refuge during life's bleakest moments. Like Abraham, we can keep going back to a place where we can be in his presence. God's presence is the ideal place to work out our worries and wrestle with our doubts and disappointments.

God, keep drawing me back into a familiar place of daily dialogue with you. Thank you for being ready to interact with my anxious thoughts.

Scripture Reading: Genesis 22-24

Obedient Faith

"God will provide a sheep for the burnt offering, my son," Abraham answered. And they both walked on together.

GENESIS 22:8 NLT

One of the most remarkable moments in the Bible is when Abraham trusts God to provide a plan of salvation for his son Isaac. As Abraham walked in obedience to God's daunting call, he leaned on God's covenant promise. After all, God had declared that Abraham would become the father of many nations, so Abraham believed that God would provide.

As a credit to Abraham's faith, God provided a sacrificial ram to take Isaac's place. Ultimately, this moment foreshadowed how God so loved the world that he would offer his only Son so that whoever believed in him would have eternal life. Jesus became the provisional sacrifice for all those who would place their trust in him.

Lord, give me the faith of Abraham. Help me trust you with my uncertainties today.

Scripture Reading: Genesis 25-27

Tyranny of Cravings

"Look, I'm dying of starvation!" said Esau. "What good is my birthright to me now?"

GENESIS 25:32 NLT

Esau famously gave up his birthright to his younger brother because he was hungry. He was ruled by his immediate desires, and the tyranny of his appetite overwhelmed him. He lost sight of the bigger picture, and he gave in to the instant gratification of filling his stomach. It seems foolish, but how often do we do the same thing?

Many of us are ruled by the idea of comfort and satisfaction. We make decisions based on how we feel in the moment, and we allow our personal gratification to rule our habits. Choosing comfort over wisdom seems good in the moment, but the long-term sacrifices aren't worth it. As followers of Jesus, we must keep our eyes on the end goal rather than doing whatever is easiest in the moment.

Lord, help me cast aside my selfish cravings in order to seek your long-term goals for my life.

Scripture Reading: Genesis 28-30

Promise Keeper

"I am with you and will keep you wherever you go, and will bring you back to this land; for I will not leave you until I have done what I have promised you."

GENESIS 28:15 NASB

God had promised Abraham a multitude of descendants through whom the whole world would be blessed. He established that blessing with Jacob. God promises to be with him, protect him, and work out his long-term plan of salvation through him. He faithfully kept his word from generation to generation.

God is a promise keeper. When he says he will do something, we can be sure he will do it. Let's lean on the integrity of the Lord's promises in Scripture. He has not forgotten what he has declared. He is faithful and trustworthy. By his mighty power, he will accomplish everything he said he would do.

Almighty God, I trust your Word. Give me confidence in your promises even when your timeline is different from my own. Fill me with your Spirit and help me remain faithful.

Scripture Reading: Genesis 31-33

Wrestling with God

"Your name will no longer be Jacob. Your name will now be Israel, because you have wrestled with God and with people, and you have won."

GENESIS 32:28 NCV

Jacob, whose name meant "heel" or "deceiver," had struggled to get his way his whole life. He held on to his twin brother's heel during their delivery and later took advantage of him during a weak moment. He schemed with his own mother to trick his father. Later in life he labored for his deceitful father-in-law and eventually fled due to their jealousy.

Jacob's whole life was contentious, so when Jacob encountered God face to face in his camp, he did what he knew best. He wrestled and fought. He insisted that God give him a blessing. That's when God changed Jacob's name to Israel which means "God Fights." Jacob was no longer supposed to fight against others but was now called to wrestle with God for God's promised blessing.

Lord, may I put my energy and effort into pursuing the blessing you have for my life rather than fighting everyone else for it.

Scripture Reading: Genesis 34-36

A Restorative Cleanse

Jacob said to his family and all who were with him, "Get rid of the foreign gods that are among you. Purify yourselves and change your clothes."

GENESIS 35:2 CSB

In preparation for God's plans, Jacob insisted that his family cleanse themselves of all offensive and sinful practices. He urged the people around him to evaluate their souls. He called them to remove anything that hindered their pursuit of the one true God.

We are all prone to giving our affections to anything and everything but God. We obsess over money, appearances, possessions, and reputations. Examining our soul can be profoundly revitalizing. It might be uncomfortable, but it will also be restorative. Taking a break from harmful habits can rid the mind of impurities and allow for sober decision-making. Ridding the soul of anything that has taken God's place will enable us to live freely without the cumbersome weight that comes from a compromised life.

Heavenly Father, forgive me for placing things in my life that do not belong to you. Cleanse me and create in me a clean heart.

Scripture Reading: Genesis 37-39

Trusting God

The LORD was with Joseph in the prison and showed him his faithful love. And the LORD made Joseph a favorite with the prison warden.

GENESIS 39:21 NLT

God sees his people in the darkness. He is present in the worst situations, and he is faithful to keep his promises. His character never changes even when we can't see what he is doing. We are called to trust his sovereignty even when the world seems to be falling apart, and it would be easier to question if he even notices. Scripture reminds us that God shows up even when suffering is great.

If you are hurting today, reach out to God. Call on him in your fear. Petition him with your frustrations. Cry to him in your despair. The same God who was present with Joseph in prison will not abandon you. He promises to work out everything for good. You can confidently trust in his great vision, perfect timing, and unfailing love.

Oh Lord, help me fully trust you in my struggles today. Be close to me and give me favor with those around me as you work out your plans.

Scripture Reading: Genesis 40-42

Reflect God

This proposal pleased Pharaoh and all his servants. And Pharaoh said to his servants, "Can we find a man like this, in whom is the Spirit of God?"

GENESIS 41:38 ESV

The way Joseph carried himself led Pharoah to recognize God. Joseph's decisions, habits, and demeanor all pointed to the God of Israel. It was clear that God was at work in his life. Similarly, we are called to live in such a way that the people around us take notice. We were not made to follow the crowd or fade into the background. We each have an opportunity to display God's character through our skills, words, actions, and attitudes.

Today, make it your aim to demonstrate qualities of the God who interprets dreams, supplies resources for those in need, comforts the anxious-hearted, and sustains the honorable. May the way you live prompt others to give God the glory he is due. You were created by God, you are held together by him, and you exist for his glory.

Lord, may your Holy Spirit direct the work of my hands and the wisdom of my words so that others will be drawn to give you glory.

Scripture Reading: Genesis 43-45

Christ Foreshadowed

"Please let your servant remain here as my lord's slave in place of the boy, and let the boy return with his brothers."
GENESIS 44:33 NIV

Judah took responsibility for the protection of his youngest brother. He had cowered long enough, and he was done following his brother's plans. He displayed courage and selflessness by being willing to sacrifice his position for his brother. He was willing to take the brunt of the punishment in order to save his father from further heartache.

Later in the book of Revelation, Jesus is described as the "Lion of the tribe of Judah." He is the one who stepped up to take the consequence of humanity's sin. He refused to let sin win. Judah's actions in Genesis foreshadowed Christ's willingness to save us from heartache by taking the punishment for our sin. Jesus was our substitute sacrifice, and he triumphed over death.

Jesus, the Lion of Judah, you are worthy of my praise. Give me courage to be selfless as I learn more about you.

Scripture Reading: Genesis 46-48

Providing for Others

Joseph gave his father, his brothers, and everyone who lived with them the food they needed.

GENESIS 47:12 NCV

One of the most profound accomplishments in the story of Joseph is that his family was saved from starvation. Joseph's father, brothers, their families had been on the brink of ruin. The famine that had devastated the entire region had brought them to their knees. There was no way they could continue on their own. The only option was to seek help from the fearsome Egyptian empire.

The hurt and hardship of Joseph's life led to a pivotal moment. His obedience to God's wisdom saved his family. The organizational skills God had given Joseph enabled God's people to be rescued and blessed. God loves using people to provide for others needs and to sustain them in times of trouble.

Lord, give me your wisdom and foresight to provide for those you have entrusted to my care.

Scripture Reading: Genesis 49-50

God's Vision

Joseph said to his brothers, "I am about to die, but God will assuredly take care of you and bring you up from this land to the land which He promised on oath to Abraham, to Isaac, and to Jacob."

GENESIS 50:24 NASB

Genesis sets the stage for God's great plan. It is the beginning of a grand story where God orchestrates a movement of salvation for humanity through a singular family. From Abraham to Isaac to Jacob, God promised to produce a line of people through whom all the nations of the world would be blessed.

Joseph, a son of Jacob, recalls God's vision on his deathbed. With his dying words he reminded his brothers of their place in the promise of God. His encouragement applies to us as well. We are asked to be faithful to the call we have received from God. He equips us to trust in his ways, follow his commands, and walk according to his long-term plan for this world.

Almighty God, don't let me forget my place in your grand plans for this world. Let me live in alignment with what you have promised to do.

Scripture Reading: Exodus 1-3

His Name

God said to Moses, "I am who I am. This is what you are to say to the Israelites: 'I am has sent me to you.'"

EXODUS 3:14 NIV

When Moses meets the Lord in person he is given a remarkable gift. God shared his name with him. By knowing God's name, Moses is given the privilege of knowing God personally. Moses is welcomed into a relationship by the God of his ancestors Abraham, Isaac, and Jacob. Moses had made many mistakes, but God still met him and fulfilled his purposes through him.

God's desire is to redeem his people and renew our purposes. He doesn't want us to live separately from him, and he doesn't want our sin to get in the way of having a relationship with him. He offers us salvation and forgiveness whenever we call upon his name.

Lord, thank you for the invitation to get to know you personally. Give me grace to serve you more purposefully today.

Scripture Reading: Exodus 4-6

God's Faithfulness

"I will claim you as my own people, and I will be your God. Then you will know that I am the LORD your God who has freed you from your oppression in Egypt."

EXODUS 6:7 NLT

The people of Israel needed regular reminders that God saw their trouble and was working to rescue them. They struggled to trust that God would do what he had promised. They had become so discouraged by the difficulty of their circumstances that they grew weary in their faith. Moses, as one of God's people, needed reminders as well. He was pessimistic as to whether he could skillfully lead people to the desired outcomes. He fought to trust himself let alone God.

Thankfully, God keeps his promises despite our potential lack of faith. He told Moses that he would rescue Israel from their bondage, and he did. His ability to stay faithful to his word doesn't depend on our strength. He is who he says he is, and he will do what he says he will do.

God, thank you for reminding me of your faithfulness. May I trust more deeply in your promises today.

Scripture Reading: Exodus 7-9

Heart Condition

The heart of Pharaoh was hardened, and he did not let the people of Israel go, just as the LORD had spoken through Moses.

EXODUS 9:35 ESV

There is a medical condition called constrictive pericarditis where hard tissue forms on the outside of the heart. This condition is life threatening because it constricts the ability of the heart to function properly. To say that Pharoah's heart was hardened implies that his ability accept God's commands was constricted. He had grown stubborn and was unwilling to see the truth.

God offers us healing and freedom through Jesus today. It's important to be mindful of the signs and to keep our hearts soft. It's our responsibility to remain willing to listen to God's instructions. May his Word be deeply rooted in our hearts as we strive to apply it even when it's uncomfortable. Following Jesus will sometimes mean saying no to our flesh, but depriving our flesh is better than hardening our hearts.

Lord, keep my heart soft toward you and your commands. Give me grace to be obedient even when I don't want to.

Scripture Reading: Exodus 10-12

A Day to Remember

"This is a day to remember. Each year, from generation to generation, you must celebrate it as a special festival to the LORD. This is a law for all time."

EXODUS 12:14 NLT

The Lord promised that if his people would mark the doors of their homes with the blood of a lamb, they would be spared the plague of death. He told them to prepare for this awful night by making a special meal. This practice of preparation would come to be known as the Passover meal, and it is still celebrated thousands of years later a remembrance of the day that God saved his people.

Jesus eventually participated in the Passover tradition. He broke bread which represented his own body being broken to free us from the bondage of sin. He poured wine which represented the blood he would shed for the forgiveness of sin. Jesus became the Passover lamb, and his sacrifice covers anyone who accepts freedom and life from God. His blood saves us from the plague of death once and for all time.

Jesus, thank you for offering me life and forgiveness through your sacrificial death on the cross. I accept you as my Savior and Lord!

Scripture Reading: Exodus 13-15

Guided by God

The LORD went ahead of them in a pillar of cloud to lead them on their way during the day and in a pillar of fire to give them light at night, so that they could travel day or night.

EXODUS 13:21 CSB

The Lord guides his people by day and night. He does not grow tired, and he does not need to take a break. He will not remove his guidance from those who follow him. If we are pursued by enemies, God will guide us to safety. If we are lost in the desert, he will lead us to refreshing waters. If we are drowning in our sin, he lifts us up and helps us heal. He is our cloud by day and our fire by night through every season of the soul.

God invites us to follow him. He calls us to surrender our plans and go wherever he leads. Not only does he ask us to trust him, but he promises to be with us every step of the way. He knows exactly where we need to go, and he will equip us with whatever we need to get there. What a privilege to pursue the Lord and trust his steps.

God, I was made to follow you. Guide me in my decisions and lead my steps.

Scripture Reading: Exodus 16-18

Trusted Supporters

Later, when Moses' arms became tired, the men put a large rock under him, and he sat on it. Then Aaron and Hur held up Moses' hands—Aaron on one side and Hur on the other. They kept his hands steady until the sun went down.

Exodus 17:12 NCV

Even Moses, as great of a leader as he was, needed help from trusted supporters. He couldn't be all things to all people all the time. He needed to entrust partners with his mission. He needed accountability, and he needed to lean on others. He grew tired because he was just a man, and the weight of responsibility was sometimes more than he could handle by himself. When he grew weary, he had faithful friends and brothers to hold him up and keep him steady.

Who are your trusted supporters? Who are the faithful men in your life? Who are the ones who will step into battle and hold up your tired arms? It is important to have reliable men in your life. No one was created to withstand the pressures of life alone. Gritting your teeth and mustering up your own strength isn't the only option. It's okay to lean on trusted friends when you are weary.

Lord, place strong men of faith in my life. May they inspire me and hold me accountable to the calling you have given me.

Scripture Reading: Exodus 19-21

Your God

"I am the LORD your God, who rescued you from the land of Egypt, the place of your slavery.
You must not have any other god but me."
EXODUS 20:2-3 NLT

God isn't an uninvolved dictator who insists that we follow him. He isn't a tyrant who wants us to follow his rules for the sake of obedience. He doesn't have an inflated ego, and he isn't power hungry. He is a kind and loving father who mindfully cares for his children. He faithfully guides us, and he intervenes on our behalf. He asks us to be faithful to him because he is always faithful to us.

God is worthy of our allegiance. His intentions toward us are good, and his purposes will always prosper. He rescues us, heals us, and offers us freedom that cannot be found anywhere else. We are not worthy of his faithfulness, yet he will never let us down. We can acknowledge the greatness of God by accepting his presence in our lives and offering him all we have.

God, I devote my life to you. Thank you for rescuing me and for guiding me so personally today.

Scripture Reading: Exodus 22-25

With Us

"Let them make me a sanctuary; that I may dwell among them."

Exodus 25:8 KJV

God longs to be close to those whom he loves. He was near to Israel as he led their Exodus from Egypt, and he instructed them to build a tabernacle so he would have a place to reside among them as they wandered the wilderness. There was never a point in their journey when he left them alone to figure out the next step. He was with them, guiding and sustaining them, from beginning to end.

We are never left alone because God has chosen to dwell with us. Christ made a way for us to be near God without hindrance or interruption. Jesus walked among us, laid down his life, and rose from the grave so we would have a way to be with God forever. Scripture reminds us that we have the constant companionship of his Spirit, and that God will draw near to us if we draw near to him. He is not distant or far off; he is always close.

Jesus, thank you for never abandoning me. Thank you for drawing near to me through your Spirit.

Scripture Reading: Exodus 26-28

Set Apart

"These are the garments that they shall make: a breastpiece, an ephod, a robe, a coat of checker work, a turban, and a sash. They shall make holy garments for Aaron your brother and his sons to serve me as priests."

Exodus 28:4 ESV

The intricate designs of the priestly garments in ancient Israel may seem odd to us today. Their purpose, however, had significant meaning. They set the priests apart from anything that was defiled or blemished. In other words, the clothing that Aaron and his sons wore became a reminder of the holiness of God.

Scripture refers to Christ's followers as a "priesthood of all believers." In effect, every follower of Jesus is called to be holy and set apart. The question before us today is will we live in holiness so that we can lead others to a close relationship with God? Each day holds the opportunity to conduct ourselves in a manner worthy of the Lord.

Heavenly Father, forgive me for my sinful thoughts and actions. Clothe me in your holiness so that I may represent you to others.

Scripture Reading: Exodus 29-31

Living with God

"I will dwell among the sons of Israel and will be their God. And they shall know that I am the LORD their God who brought them out of the land of Egypt, so that I might dwell among them; I am the LORD their God."

EXODUS 29:45-46 NASB

Scripture emphasizes that God intended to live among his people. It was his goal from Creation onward. He wanted to know Adam and Eve. He wanted to walk with Noah. He wanted to talk to Abraham. He wanted to be face-to-face with Moses. God wants relationship with his people.

It is not surprising that God wants to be with us today. He does not want to be an appointment on our calendars or become an item on our to-do lists. He does not enjoy being treated like a dental visit, business lunch, or an oil change. God is here with us right now, beckoning us to acknowledge his presence and share life with him. Let's invite him into the details of our days and walk alongside him wherever we go.

Lord, be my constant companion throughout this day. Give me grace to turn my gaze toward you moment by moment.

Scripture Reading: Exodus 32-34

Speaking with God

The LORD would speak with Moses face to face, just as a man speaks with his friend, then Moses would return to the camp. His assistant, the young man Joshua son of Nun, would not leave the inside of the tent.

EXODUS 33:11 CSB

The relationship Moses had with God was noteworthy because it was close and personal. Many people witnessed the great miracles of Exodus but still saw God as mysterious or detached. They potentially saw him as the massive cloud of smoke or pillar of fire that led them along their journey. The idea of drawing near to God would have been a daunting concept.

Moses encountered God in a personal way many times. He grew to desire his presence, long for his counsel, and yearn for his Spirit. He cultivated a relationship with him, and he taught those who came after him to do the same. He demonstrated what it looked like to have a faith-filled relationship with God, and we still look to him as an example.

God, I want to know you in such a way that those around me can see that I have been with you. Let the genuineness of our relationship impact others for years to come.

Scripture Reading: Exodus 35-37

Using Your Gifts

"See, the LORD has chosen Bezalel son of Uri, the son of Hur, of the tribe of Judah, and he has filled him with the Spirit of God, with wisdom, with understanding, with knowledge and with all kinds of skills."

EXODUS 35:30-31 NIV

The Lord loves calling people to use their gifts to do wonderful things. He made each person unique, and he calls us to work together to bless the world. In Exodus we see that God used the skills and talents of a craftsman named Bezalel to bless the nation of Israel. Over the course of several chapters there is a detailed account of Bezalel's work. His story reveals that God is glorified when we use the gifts he's given us.

What do you love to do? What activity fills your heart? What skills do others notice in you? The answers to those questions are not arbitrary. God made you in a particular way on purpose. You have permission to thrive in the ways that he created you. Using your gifts is an act of worship toward the Lord, and it is a great blessing to the people around you.

Lord, use my passions and skills to benefit others and bring glory to your name.

Scripture Reading: Exodus 38-40

Journey with God

Whenever the cloud lifted from the Tabernacle, the people of Israel would set out on their journey, following it.

Exodus 40:36 NLT

God led the people through the desert as a cloud by day and a pillar of fire by night. When the cloud lifted, the people would move. They would not pack up and depart before the cloud had lifted. They didn't just get up and go whenever they felt like it. Israel had learned that if they stopped following God to pursue their own concocted strategies, their efforts would backfire.

Learning how to follow God's leadership is a pursuit worthy of your entire life. There might be times when you have a misstep, but he promises to keep you steady if your eyes are on him. He offers you his faithful presence, and he will not let you down. So, where is God leading you today? Has God started moving and called for you to join him?

Lord, I will follow you all the days of my life. Guide me on the path you've chosen. Help me be responsive to your leadership.

Scripture Reading: Leviticus 1-3

Eternal Sacrifice

"If you offer a lamb, you are to present it before the LORD, lay your hand on its head and slaughter it in front of the tent of meeting. Then Aaron's sons shall splash its blood against the sides of the altar."

LEVITICUS 3:7-8 NIV

The sacrifices offered by the priests of Israel established a way for God's people to routinely show reverence and ask for forgiveness. In the case of the peace offering a person would select a lamb without defect and present it to the priests. That person would lay his hand on the head of the animal signifying that the animal would be taking his place as the recipient of judgment.

We no longer operate under a priestly system. We aren't required to make sacrifices or atone for our sins. This is because Jesus is our eternal sacrifice. His death and resurrection paid the price for our sins. We surrender our lives at the foot of the cross, trust the Spirit to guide us, and set our hope upon the day that he returns.

Jesus, Lamb of God, thank you for offering your own life as the final and complete sacrifice for the forgiveness of my sin.

February

"The grass withers, the flowers fade,
but the word of our God remains forever."

Isaiah 40:8 CSB

Scripture Reading: Leviticus 4-6

Notice and Confess

"When you become aware of your guilt in any of these ways, you must confess your sin."
LEVITICUS 5:5 NLT

God has always expected people to admit their sin once they realize their guilt. Scripture promises that if a person confesses their sin, God is faithful and just. He will forgive them and cleanse them from all unrighteousness. That is good news! Sin causes separation from a holy, perfect God, yet God longs to be in eternal relationship with his people. He mercifully provides an anthem of restoration in the words of the guilty one who would proclaim, "I have sinned." God is pleased to forgive the soul who calls on him for salvation in this way.

Jesus offered his life and shed his blood to be the once-for-all substitutionary sacrifice for our sins. When we confess and call on his name, we will be freed from the burden of guilt. He longs for us to give him our worries, struggles, failures, and fears. We each get to decide if our awareness of our sin will create shame or an opportunity for freedom.

Jesus, thank you for dying on the cross to rescue a sinner like me.

Scripture Reading: Leviticus 7-9

At the Altar

"Come to the altar and sacrifice your sin offering and your burnt offering to purify yourself and the people. Then present the offerings of the people to purify them, making them right with the LORD, just as he has commanded."

LEVITICUS 9:7 NLT

Moses beckoned Aaron to come to the altar. In Israel's system of sacrifice, the altar was the place where God's people could gather to seek purification from sin and reconciliation with God. It was the location where they could offer a sacrifice of praise in the presence of God.

Today, God still prompts us to come to the altar, but now the altar is the Cross of Christ. Jesus was presented as the sin offering for anyone who would accept his sacrifice on their behalf. We are beckoned to seek him at the Cross and find his arms open wide, carrying our sin on his shoulders and offering us forgiveness and redemption through his sacrifice.

Jesus, I come to the altar of your Cross today. May I live in the freedom you have given me.

Scripture Reading: Leviticus 10-12

Will of God

"You must distinguish between the holy and the common, and the clean and the unclean, and teach the Israelites all the statutes that the LORD has given to them through Moses."

LEVITICUS 10:10-11 CSB

The Lord wanted Aaron and his sons to be set apart from the unclean practices of their day. He wanted them to live missionally, always considering how their habits and commitments represented God's ways to those around them. The Lord instructed them to distinguish between the holy and the common. He wanted them to know the difference between what was considered clean and unclean.

We are surrounded by opportunities to compromise and lower our standards. There are ample enticements seducing us to participate in ungodly activities and to settle into ungodly thoughts. It's important in this clouded culture to be able to clearly discern right from wrong. Learning to live wisely today requires us to seek the counsel of the Holy Spirit so we can live in accordance with his commands.

Lord, give me the insight and wisdom that I need to see what is good and to act according to your will. Help me follow the guidance of the Holy Spirit in all I do.

Scripture Reading: Leviticus 13-15

Hope for Suffering

"The priest who cleanses him shall set the man who is to be cleansed and these things before the LORD, at the entrance of the tent of meeting."

LEVITICUS 14:11 ESV

These chapters in Leviticus are not the most cited passages of Scripture. They are not the sections of the Bible selected for motivational posters or memorized as favorite verses. They are not considered the most inspiring of passages. Instead, these chapters can cause readers of the Old Testament to cringe, squirm, and look away. They are chapters dealing with hygienic practices, skin infections, diseases, and awkward sexual situations.

The Old Testament is a picture of how much God cared for his people. He cared about people who suffered from conditions that made life miserable and unmanageable. He cared about people who became ostracized due to medical illness or who got caught up in unhealthy habits. He didn't like what diseases and devastation did to people's lives, so he instituted a series of instructions on how to deal with each situation.

Lord, thank you for offering healing and hope in every situation. Restore me to wholeness and help me show others who you are.

Scripture Reading: Leviticus 16-18

The Scapegoat

"The goat chosen by lot as the scapegoat shall be presented alive before the LORD to be used for making atonement by sending it into the wilderness as a scapegoat."

LEVITICUS 16:10 NIV

The term "scapegoat" is used in our culture today to describe someone who takes the fall for the mistakes or sins of others. Instead of punishing the ones who committed bad deeds, an innocent person receives the judgment. The guilty people escape the consequence of their actions because the penalty is placed on someone else.

This term originates from the book of Leviticus. The priests would choose a goat which would symbolically carry the sins of the people away into the wilderness. The priest would lay both of his hands on the goat and confess the sins of the Israelites. This powerful symbolic act was ultimately demonstrated through Jesus, who became the scapegoat for all people. Those who confess their sin will escape consequence because their sin has been laid on Jesus, and he carries it away.

Jesus, I have sinned and fallen short of your glory. I do not deserve to escape the consequence of my actions. Thank you for saving me by taking my sin upon yourself.

Scripture Reading: Leviticus 19-21

Be Holy

"You shall be holy, for I the Lord your God am holy."
Leviticus 19:2 ESV

God wants us to be holy because holiness reflects his nature. We were created in the image of a holy God. We don't need to be intimidated by this call because he has shown us what it looks like to live a holy life. He hasn't left us without instruction or guidance. He calls us to live up to his standard, and he graciously equips us to do it.

God wants us to be holy because holiness is good for us and others. Life is better when we do what is right, admirable, and trustworthy. When we make right choices with our attitudes and behavior, our resiliency is strengthened, and we grow in character. God's instructions benefit all who follow them.

God, empower me by your Spirit to be holy in my actions today. May I live for your glory and for the benefit of those around me.

Scripture Reading: Leviticus 22-24

Time to Rest

"You have six days each week for your ordinary work, but the seventh day is a Sabbath day of complete rest, an official day for holy assembly. It is the LORD's Sabbath day, and it must be observed wherever you live."

LEVITICUS 23:3 NLT

Throughout the year God established intentional times for the people of Israel to set aside their regular routines in order to focus on him. There were major seasonal festivals such as Passover, Harvest, or the Feast of Tabernacles. Each one recognized different aspects of Israel's relationship with God. They were an opportunity to pause, gather, and remember what God had done.

God didn't want people to passively wait for these festivals as the only reminders of his faithfulness. He also intended for his people to set aside time for weekly rest through the Sabbath. Every seventh day God wanted his people to recognize the restoration that only he could provide. This habit is still available to us today. There is peace and encouragement found by setting aside our work, gathering together, and remembering God's goodness.

Lord, may I see the wisdom and beauty of the rhythms you have established. May my life reflect what you desire.

Scripture Reading: Leviticus 25-27

Time of Jubilee

"Make the fiftieth year a special year, and announce freedom for all the people living in your country. This time will be called Jubilee. You will each go back to your own property, each to your own family and family group."

LEVITICUS 25:10 NCV

The year of Jubilee was meant to be an extension of the weekly Sabbath. It was an entire year devoted to rest and restoration. It was a time for the people and the land they worked to be restored. God's system allowed for fair and honest transactions, and it prevented an unequal distribution of wealth.

The practices God instilled in the Old Testament give us a glimpse into his character. We serve a God who cares about his people. He cares about the work we do and how it impacts us. He sees our struggles, and he is not blind to our toil. While the world seems horrible out of balance now, we can look forward to a time when everything will be restored.

Heavenly Father, help me reflect the values of Jubilee in my actions today. Help me act responsibly and to show dignity to everyone I meet.

Scripture Reading: Numbers 1-3

Set up Camp

The sons of Israel did all this; according to all that the LORD commanded Moses, so they camped by their flags, and so they set out, everyone by his family according to his father's household.

NUMBERS 2:34 NASB

The book of Numbers offers an interesting perspective of Israel's history. They spent years wandering in the wilderness, and they were instructed never to settle into a permanent location. They escaped slavery in Egypt, and they eagerly anticipated arriving home in the land God had given their ancestor Abraham. They lived nomadic lives while they waited for God to lead them home.

God was their home while they wandered. He was their source of belonging and identity. They could not find security in their possession or their location, so God urged them to depend on him for every step of their journey. They held all things loosely except for their faith in the one who was leading them. Their allegiance to God was the most important priority of their lives, so they strove to follow everything he commanded.

Lord, let me find my identity and contentment in you above everything else. Be the focus of my goals and pursuits today.

Scripture Reading: Numbers 4-6

Give This Blessing

"The Lord bless you
and keep you;
the Lord make his face shine on you
and be gracious to you;
the Lord turn his face toward you
and give you peace."

Numbers 6:24-26 niv

The Lord instructed Aaron and his sons to speak over the people of Israel. They were informed that whenever they would give this blessing to God's people then they too would be blessed by God. When they declared God's character and intentions, he was faithful to include them in his blessing.

God wants his people to be blessed. He wants to keep, protect, hold, and look out for us. He wants his face to shine upon us as we go about our lives. His intentions toward us are good and kind. He is a mindful father who delights in his children. He longs to be involved, and he beams with pride as we follow him.

God, remind me of your graciousness toward me. Remind me throughout the day to pray this blessing for the people in my life.

Scripture Reading: Numbers 7-9

Inviting Others

"If foreigners living among you want to celebrate the Passover to the LORD, they must follow these same decrees and regulations."

NUMBERS 9:14 NLT

In the first year after the Exodus from Egypt, the Israelites wandered in the wilderness. They established various guidelines and practices that would define them as a nation. After spending hundreds of years enslaved in another country, one might suspect their new laws would be vindictive or self-protective against foreigners. Remarkably, by the gracious instruction of God, Israel's governing rules were inclusionary toward foreigners who lived among them.

Throughout the Old Testament, the people of Israel remembered the harsh treatment they suffered as strangers in a foreign land. At the inception of their nation, the people of God did not want to be guilty of treating foreigners the way Egypt had. God equipped them to be gracious and kind even when their experiences could have warranted isolation and self-preservation.

Lord, may I have a posture of invitation toward others. Help me be kind and inclusive so those who don't know you might come to follow you.

Scripture Reading: Numbers 10-12

The Complaining Heart

The people complained about their hardships in the hearing of the LORD, and when he heard them his anger was aroused. Then fire from the LORD burned among them and consumed some of the outskirts of the camp.

NUMBERS 11:1 NIV

God faithfully led the Israelites out of captivity, but their response toward him wasn't always thankful. They grumbled and complained even though they had countless reasons to confidently praise God for all he'd done. They had seen his miracles with their own eyes, experienced his daily provision, and followed him through the wilderness. God was present with them every step of the way, yet they still grumbled and stubbornly resisted his leadership at times.

We can use the Israelites unflattering behavior as a mirror for our own hearts. How often do we experience God's goodness and choose complaint? How often do we reap the benefits of his generosity and grumble before the memory of our blessing has even faded? Like the Israelites, we can also learn to intentionally thank God. We can declare his goodness and deliberately take notice of his good work.

Lord, convict me of my selfish, grumbling attitude. Don't let me take all that you have done for granted.

Scripture Reading: Numbers 13-15

Faith of Caleb

Caleb quieted the people before Moses and said, "Let us go up at once and occupy it, for we are well able to overcome it."

NUMBERS 13:30 ESV

As nearly everyone else cowered in fear, a young leader named Caleb stood boldly in his conviction. He knew that God could do what he said he would do. All the people had to do was follow the path God had set for them. Caleb eagerly trusted that the Lord would deliver them into the Promised Land. The strength and size of the enemies in the way caused great anxiety to the others, but Caleb knew that God was more than able to accomplish his plans.

Caleb's faith greatly impacted Joshua who was a young leader in the new nation. He and Caleb remained resolute in the face of opposition, and they urged everyone around them to trust in God. The other men reacted with panic and violence to the impending threats, but Caleb and Joshua were vindicated as God intervened and rescued them.

Lord, let me stand boldly in my faith today even when those around me shrink in fear. Give me strength to lean on you.

Scripture Reading: Numbers 16-18

Gift of Tithing

"When you receive from the Israelites the tenth that I have given you as your inheritance, you are to present part of it as an offering to the LORD—a tenth of the tenth."

NUMBERS 18:26 CSB

Tithing was considered part of the Israelite's law. It was the practice of giving the first ten percent of their belongings as an act of sacrifice. It was acknowledgement that God had generously provided all they needed and more. Tithing was a physical reminder to humbly express gratitude to God for his loving provision. It also offered practical support to the priests who were managing the system of religious practices.

There is no specific indication that tithing remains a rule or law for Christians today, but the principle certainly remains. The New Testament teaches us to live generously rather than clinging to our possessions. We are called to keep our hands open and be willing to support those in need. This life is meant for more than gathering as much wealth as we can for ourselves.

God, thank you for providing all that I need. May I hold loosely to my belongings and faithfully support my church today.

Scripture Reading: Numbers 19-21

Actions and Attitudes

Moses raised his hand and struck the rock twice with the staff, and water gushed out. So the entire community and their livestock drank their fill.

NUMBERS 20:11 NLT

The Israelites were tired and thirsty as they wandered in the wilderness. In their frustration and exhaustion, they rebelled. They blamed Moses and Aaron for leading them out of slavery into the desert where there was no water. Moses and Aaron fell face down before the Lord and prayed. God appeared to the two men and provided a solution to the problem. He told Moses that he would provide water from a rock.

Moses did as God directed, but instead of speaking to the rock, Moses shouted at the people. He was obedient, but he served in anger rather than wonder and fear of the Lord. We can take note of God's reaction toward him and pay attention to not just our actions but the state of our hearts. Our attitudes matter as much as our ability to follow directions.

Lord, unchain me from the hold anger has in my heart. Soften my heart and transform my attitude along with my actions.

Scripture Reading: Numbers 22-24

Under Pressure

Balaam answered and said to the servants of Balak, "Though Balak were to give me his house full of silver and gold, I could not go beyond the command of the LORD my God to do less or more."

NUMBERS 22:18 ESV

The Israelites had been rescued from slavery and were now on the march. Their numbers were intimidating to the various kings of the area. The king of Moab in particular was threatened by the possibility of war. He instructed Balaam, a wicked prophet, to pronounce a curse upon the Israelites.

After seeking God's opinion on the matter, Balaam informed his king that the Lord would be on Israel's side. The king sent a flattering delegation of impressive people to Balaam and insisted a second time that Balaam curse the Israelites. Balaam refused again. No amount of money could tempt him to make a pronouncement that went against the Lord. For at least this moment, Balaam stood strong against the pressure.

God, may the conversations I have and the actions I take be honoring to you. Help me stand strong no matter what pressure I face.

Scripture Reading: Numbers 25-27

Transfer Your Authority

"Transfer some of your authority to him so the whole community of Israel will obey him."
NUMBERS 27:20 NLT

God led Moses to the top of a mountain that looked westward over the Jordan River toward the Promised Land. Moses knew he would die before the Israelites would settle there, and he understood that Israel needed a new leader. He asked God to appoint someone to take his place so the Israelites wouldn't suffer under a lack of leadership.

It was wise and unselfish of Moses to consider the wellbeing of the generation that would come after his time in leadership. We are wise when we do the same. We show maturity, humility, and foresight when we think about who will replace us. Will there be a gap left by our absence because we insisted on carrying a burden of leadership alone? Or will the work of the Lord continue seamlessly because we prepared for a successful future?

Lord, let me be forward thinking. Raise up others around me to carry on what you have started through me. Help me be faithful and unselfish to the end.

Scripture Reading: Numbers 28-30

Honor Your Word

"When a man makes a vow to the LORD or takes an oath to obligate himself by a pledge, he must not break his word but must do everything he said."

NUMBERS 30:2 NIV

A society will crumble when men fail to keep their word. A marriage will fall apart when a husband breaks his promises. A father's influence will wane when he doesn't show up. A business deal will collapse when a man can't be trusted. Likewise, a man who talks with integrity builds healthy communities. A man who keeps his vows builds a strong marriage. A man who remains committed to his children builds a generational legacy. A man who follows through on his promises builds a successful career.

As men of God, we are called to honor our vows. We should follow through with our commitments and be faithful to our promises. We should pay attention to our words and strive to be reliable and trustworthy. We reflect God's character when we grow in integrity. We honor his Word when we keep our word.

Heavenly Father, let my yes be yes and my no be no. Deepen my conviction to be a man of integrity today.

Scripture Reading: Numbers 31-33

Keep Track

At the LORD's direction, Moses kept a written record of their progress. These are the stages of their march, identified by the different places where they stopped along the way.

NUMBERS 33:2 NLT

God wanted Moses to keep a record of all he had done during the Exodus. After Israel escaped from Pharoah's clutches and while they wandered in the desert, Moses wrote observations about the experiences they had. He took notes about the monumental and the mundane moments in order to highlight how God had led them to freedom and guided them to the Promised Land.

God knows that we are prone to forget all he has done. He knows that time, distance, and distractions cause us to forget his faithful hand in our lives. He knows that we are prone to drift away from our convictions and our relationship with him. Through Scripture we can see that he urges us to keep track of his goodness. As we intentionally record the ways he shows up, we are less likely to forget his faithfulness.

Lord, may I never forget what you have done in my life. Thank you for leading me forward and thank you for reminding me of your faithfulness.

Scripture Reading: Numbers 34-36

Honor the Land

"You shall not defile the land in which you live, in the midst of which I dwell; for I the LORD am dwelling in the midst of the sons of Israel."

NUMBERS 35:34 NASB

God meant for the Promised Land to be a land of peace. It is, as God had told Abraham, the place from which the entire world would be blessed. It is the place where the Messiah would be born and offer salvation for anyone who calls on the name of the Lord. It is where his throne would be established and from which his reign would emanate to all corners of the earth.

It is understandable that God would command his people to do nothing that would defile the land. The land was too sacred, too special, and too important for any man to do anything contrary to the holiness of God. Perhaps today it is appropriate to consider the place in which God has called each of us to dwell. How are we honoring the space God has given us?

Lord, may my life reflect your holiness. Thank you for dwelling with me. Help me honor you so that you can move freely in my life.

Scripture Reading: Deuteronomy 1-3

A Bittersweet Prayer

"Please let me cross the Jordan to see the wonderful land on the other side, the beautiful hill country and the Lebanon mountains."

DEUTERONOMY 3:25 NLT

Moses longed to see the Promised Land, but he also knew he would not cross the Jordan River to enter the land. He faithfully led the Israelites, knowing that he wouldn't see the fulfillment of God's promise. He did his best to honor God's instructions even though he wouldn't reap the reward. Toward the end of his life this made his heart ache.

We've all yearned for something we'll never receive. It's important to recognize that we aren't alone in our longing. Following God doesn't necessarily mean we get what we want. Some dreams don't come true, yet God's faithfulness doesn't change. Some prayers won't be answered how we'd like, yet God is present through our heart ache. We don't follow him because he gives us our way; we follow him because he is worthy.

Heavenly Father, may I always lift my heart to you and may I always bend my will to yours.

Scripture Reading: Deuteronomy 4-6

Your Path

"Walk in obedience to all that the LORD your God has commanded you, so that you may live and prosper and prolong your days in the land that you will possess."

DEUTERONOMY 5:33 NIV

Each of us walks a different path through life. It's filled with unique challenges, unexpected trauma, beautiful blessings, and mundane details. We can't compare our journeys, and we can't gauge our failures and successes by our own perspective. Our circumstances are not meant to dictate our faithfulness. The twists and turns of our stories are too different, but the overarching calling is the same. We are each called to walk in obedience to all that God has commanded us.

God offers blessings along with obedience. He reminds us throughout Scripture that when we listen to him, we will prosper. The way that is executed in our individual lives may look different, but we can trust that his plans for each of us are good. Let's keep our eyes on him instead of focusing on the perceived failures and successes of the people around us.

Lord, I place my complete trust in your guidance to lead me through the unexpected journey ahead. Thank you for your faithfulness.

Scripture Reading: Deuteronomy 7-9

Claimed and Chosen

The Lord did not care for you and choose you because there were many of you—you are the smallest nation of all.
Deuteronomy 7:7 NCV

God told Israel they were a holy people who belonged to him. They were God's chosen treasure out of all the people on earth. They had not attained that designation due to their extraordinary accomplishments. They weren't the most impressive group of people on earth by any means. The size of their population certainly wasn't large enough to make the God who created the universe swoon over them. No, Israel was chosen to be treasured by God simply because he loved them and had promised himself to them.

We're told later in the New Testament that we who belong Jesus are God's chosen treasure. He has claimed us as his very own. There is nothing we can do to earn our status. We cannot capture his affection further by being better, stronger, or smarter. We are treasured simply because God loves us.

God, I am undeserving of the love you have for me. Help me live today with the confidence of knowing that you treasure me.

Scripture Reading: Deuteronomy 10-12

Modeling Faith

"You shall teach them to your children, talking of them when you are sitting in your house, and when you are walking by the way, and when you lie down, and when you rise."

DEUTERONOMY 11:19 ESV

This is not the first time in the book of Deuteronomy that God's people are challenged to examine whether their everyday practices would equip the next generations to live for the Lord. Earlier in Deuteronomy the Israelites were given the Greatest Commandment. They were told to love the Lord with all their heart, soul, and strength. That was immediately followed up with a command to model that kind of all-in faith for their children.

Many people today fail to consider the impact their behaviors have on the next generation, yet God is clear that we are responsible for passing on his principles and purposes. He asks us to saturate our daily activities with his truth. He wants us to fill our lives with evidence of his love and character in such a way that those who come after us will be blessed.

Lord, help me be more deliberate about modeling a strong faith in you so that others will be encouraged to do the same. Teach me how to honor you in the most mundane tasks.

Scripture Reading: Deuteronomy 13-15

Open-handed

"If there are any poor Israelites in your towns when you arrive in the land the LORD your God is giving you, do not be hard-hearted or tightfisted toward them. Instead, be generous and lend them whatever they need."

DEUTERONOMY 15:7-8 NLT

God gave Israel various principles to live by as they prepared to enter the Promised Land. Among them was the instruction to embrace open-handed generosity. God wanted them to offer his gracious blessings and provision to everyone even though they had once been oppressed. He didn't want them to use their negative history as a reason for being closed off and unwelcoming.

God's command for us is still the same. He asks us to be open-handed and soft-hearted toward those in need. We are thoughtful toward strangers out of allegiance to the one true God. We choose kindness over violence, compassion over judgment, and selflessness over personal power. These behaviors and attitudes set us apart as followers of the Lord.

God, loosen my clenched fists and scrape away any hardness of heart. May I live a life of generosity in all of my thoughts and actions.

Scripture Reading: Deuteronomy 16-18

Daily Devotions

"He must always keep that copy with him and read it daily as long as he lives. That way he will learn to fear the LORD his God by obeying all the terms of these instructions and decrees."

DEUTERONOMY 17:19 NLT

God knew that one day the Israelites would choose a king. He knew that they would choose to follow a man over himself. He saw the future clearly, and he graciously gave them some advice. He urged them to choose a king who wasn't selfish or power hungry. He encouraged them to choose a king who would ultimately lead their hearts closer to God. He elevated the practice of daily devotion, and he told the Israelites that their king should prioritize honoring the Lord.

We tend to be impressed by leaders who have flashy personalities and follow a particular set of rules. Like the Israelites, we will find ourselves disappointed if our measure of success doesn't match up with God's. A godly leader prioritizes daily interaction with the one true God. Policies, procedures, and impressive oration are meant to be secondary to walking humbly with God.

Lord, let me keep your Word close to my heart every day so that I will follow your commands and establish a foundation of life.

Scripture Reading: Deuteronomy 19-21

Faithful Witness

"One witness is not enough to convict anyone accused of any crime or offense they may have committed. A matter must be established by the testimony of two or three witnesses."

Deuteronomy 19:15 NIV

Ancient Israel's court system was remarkably advanced. Both prosecution and defense relied upon the voices of witnesses. Multiple people needed to validate or corroborate the situation at hand. This is a reminder to us that God values truth, proper processes, and fairness. He is not a flippant God who declares anyone guilty on a whim.

We are blessed because Jesus is our faithful witness. He stands firmly between us and God. When we give him our sins, he says that we are blameless. He advocates to the Judge that we are innocent and worthy of eternal life. He pays our debts, and he shields us from accusation. His testimony determines our fate, and he is trustworthy and good.

Jesus, thank you for standing up for me in my time of judgment. Help me live fully in the freedom you have won for me.

Scripture Reading: Deuteronomy 22-24

Repeated Themes

"Never take advantage of poor and destitute laborers, whether they are fellow Israelites or foreigners living in your towns."

DEUTERONOMY 24:14 NLT

Scripture is full of repeated themes. We can view these as unnecessary repetitions, or we can assume that their redundancy is meant to prove a point. In the twenty-fourth chapter of Deuteronomy one of these repeated themes is on display. The nation of Israel is called to establish regulations that protect the vulnerable and give them an opportunity to pursue success. God urges his people to reflect his character in this way. It is a groundbreaking establishment of labor laws and human rights.

If we consider that repeated themes relay importance and emphasis, we can assume that God cares deeply about the vulnerable. We can put two and two together and confidently declare that God is mindful of those who are hurting. He is aware of those who are oppressed and treated unfairly, and he wants our policies to reflect that awareness. He wants his character to sink into our opinions and practices.

Lord, give me greater understanding of your character. Help me model my life after your values and purposes.

March

I have treasured your word in my heart
so that I may not sin against you.

Psalm 119:11 csb

Scripture Reading: Deuteronomy 25-27

Listen and Obey

"You shall obey the LORD your God, and do His commandments and His statutes which I am commanding you today."

DEUTERONOMY 27:10 NASB

Perhaps the most repeated theme in the first five books of the Bible is the theme of obedience to God's commandments. The concept of obedience is used hundreds of times in these first five books, and thousands of times throughout the Bible. From beginning to end we are taught that following God means listening to what he says and shaping our lives after his commands.

Jesus highlighted obedience in his ministry when he commissioned his disciples to make disciples. He asks us to teach everyone how to obey God's commands. Obedience is paramount to our faith. We cannot say we are following God while refusing to adjust our personal lives. We cannot lead others to the joy of honoring the Lord if we ourselves are flippant about his instructions.

Lord, I need to take the concept of obedience more seriously in my life. Search me and point out anything in me that offends you. Help me listen and respond to your commands.

Scripture Reading: Deuteronomy 28-30

Focus on Obedience

"You must completely obey the LORD your God, and you must carefully follow all his commands I am giving you today. Then the LORD your God will make you greater than any other nation on earth."

DEUTERONOMY 28:1 NCV

Some people try to become great by pursuing their own glory and obeying their own desires. Some people justify cutting corners and cheating systems in their accumulation of wealth and power. They hurt people as they pursue their goals with little regard to how their actions impact others. This selfish pursuit of grandeur is an arrogant, lonely way to live. Becoming great on this path relies on creating a wake of destruction.

God sets a different path to greatness. He promised that Israel would become the greatest nation on earth, and he called them to be a source of blessing and salvation for all people. He didn't ask them to pursue might or power; he asked them to live obediently to his Word. His definition of greatness requires denial of self and obedience to his ways over our own.

Lord, why do I strive for my own personal gain? Help me pursue you and your ways today.

Scripture Reading: Deuteronomy 31-34

Proclaim and Ascribe

"I will proclaim the name of the LORD;
Ascribe greatness to our God!"
DEUTERONOMY 32:3 ESV

The English word proclaim means to publicly declare or announce something that is important and needs to be emphasized. To proclaim the name of the Lord means to call attention to God. It means to put emphasis on God and his role in our lives. We proclaim his name by declaring the truth about his character and announcing to all who will listen that his name is above all other names.

To ascribe means to give someone the credit they deserve. It means to attribute a quality to whom it belongs. To ascribe greatness to our God means recognizing that he alone is great. It means acknowledging that he is the source of all things, and he is always good. When we follow this formula of proclaiming and ascribing, our hearts will soften in worship toward the one true God.

Heavenly Father, help me proclaim your name and ascribe greatness to you. May I promote your name and your greatness above all else.

Scripture Reading: Joshua 1-3

Always with Us

"Have I not commanded you? Be strong and courageous. Do not be afraid; do not be discouraged, for the LORD your God will be with you wherever you go."

JOSHUA 1:9 NIV

As Joshua prepared to lead the nation of Israel into the Promised Land after years of wandering in the wilderness, he must have had a knot in his stomach. He was likely nervous, yet he was going to do what God had planned for him to do. God took this opportunity to reassure him of a powerful truth. He reminded him of his faithful presence, and he encouraged him to be strong.

God extends the same promise toward us no matter what we are facing. His encouragement is just as applicable for our lives as it was for Joshua. Our battles are not more or less difficult than the ones he encountered. If God was faithful then, he will be faithful now. If he offered strength to his people then, he offers strength and courage to us now.

God, walk with me through everything I face today. Thank you for being faithful through it all.

Scripture Reading: Joshua 4-6

Building Memorials

"We will use these stones to build a memorial. In the future your children will ask you, 'What do these stones mean?'"

JOSHUA 4:6 NLT

The Israelites had just crossed the Jordan River into the Promised Land. The miraculous crossing was reminiscent of the way God had parted the Red Sea. Upon crossing, God told Joshua to collect twelve stones from the middle of the dry riverbed and then carry them to their new camp. Each stone represented one of the twelve tribes of Israel, and they were instructed to build a memorial with them. This would remind future generations God's faithfulness.

When Joshua built the stone memorial, his intention was that generations of people would ask what it was for. The hope was that their curiosity would lead them to understand and experience God's faithfulness for themselves. Our habit of building memorials in our lives can do the same thing. As we deliberately take note of what God has done, the people around us will see his goodness displayed in our lives.

Lord, show me what I could set up today as a reminder to others of all you have done in my life.

Scripture Reading: Joshua 7-9

Seek the Lord

The men took some of their provisions, but did not ask counsel from the LORD.

JOSHUA 9:14 ESV

One of Israel's first mistakes in the Promised Land was to make a significant decision without consulting God. The decision seemed good from their own perspective, so they didn't even think to pray about it or seek the Lord's opinion. Simply put, they neglected to consider God in their course of action. This resulted in a negative outcome because they were limited by their own perspective.

Life is filled with significant decisions. We all have choices to make, and we all need wisdom to do the right thing. Seeking God's counsel shows wisdom and maturity. It takes humility to admit that we don't have all the answers, and we can't see all the intricate details of the big picture. When we ask God for discernment, he is happy to lead us along the right path. When we consult him in prayer, he is pleased to give us the direction we need.

Lord, don't let me lean on my own wisdom for the important decisions I need to make. I need your guidance.

Scripture Reading: Joshua 10-12

Modeling Leadership

As the LORD had commanded his servant Moses, so Moses commanded Joshua. And Joshua did as he was told, carefully obeying all the commands that the LORD had given to Moses.

JOSHUA 11:15 NLT

One of the reasons Joshua was such an inspirational and successful leader is that he had been an apprentice of another inspirational, successful leader. Joshua had been mentored by one of the greatest leaders in world history. He watched Moses overcome gigantic obstacles and navigate sticky situations with proficient skill and genuine integrity. Most profoundly, Joshua had seen Moses model a lifestyle of obedience to God through it all.

Like Joshua, we are blessed when we look for godly examples to follow. It is wise to find people we admire and can look up to. As we humbly learn from each other, we can display a fuller picture of God's character. We can learn from each other's strengths, and we can help each other with our weaknesses.

God, help me be intentional about who I am being influenced by and who I am influencing.

Scripture Reading: Joshua 13-15

Faithful Example

"Just as the LORD promised, he has kept me alive for forty-five years since the time he said this to Moses, while Israel moved about in the wilderness. So here I am today, eighty-five years old!"

JOSHUA 14:10 NIV

Caleb was a faithful soldier, leader, and friend. He knew the mission, and he never wavered. Caleb's commitment to God was uncompromised for forty years. His long track record of integrity and reliability was a testimony to God's faithfulness. When others panicked, Caleb trusted God and spoke up on behalf of God's promises. When others cowered, Caleb was empowered by God's Spirit to accomplish great things.

Some of us have "Calebs" in our own lives. We have had the joyous opportunity to watch men of God live their lives with integrity and honor. We have seen them follow the Lord all of their days, and we have been blessed by their faithfulness. Let's make sure that we celebrate them!

Lord, thank you for the men in my life who have been faithful to you. Thank you for the example they've set for me. May I honor them today and bring glory to your name.

Scripture Reading: Joshua 16-18

Easily Entangled

The descendants of Manasseh could not possess these cities, because the Canaanites were determined to stay in this land.

JOSHUA 17:12 CSB

The tribe of Manasseh was up against a grating challenge. They faced a determined enemy who dug in and became a constant thorn in their side. Instead of trusting the Lord and his power, Manasseh struggled to overcome their persistent enemy. As time went on, the nagging presence of the pagan practices of the Canaanites eventually caused the people of Manasseh to lose sight of God and to be caught up in the thickets of sin.

This situation is not uncommon. If we read Hebrews, we'll see that we are encouraged to rid ourselves of things that would easily entangle our morals and eventually compromise our pursuit of Jesus. God knows that many temptations will come our way, and he equips us to remain faithful despite them. The lesson to us is to remain focused on the call that Jesus has given us and to run unhindered in our commitment to purity and righteousness.

Lord, forgive me for not expelling lurking sins from my life. Give me courage of faith to cast my temptations and burdens upon you.

Scripture Reading: Joshua 19-21

God Follows Through

Not one of the good promises which the LORD had made to the house of Israel failed; everything came to pass.
JOSHUA 21:45 NASB

Scripture is filled with God's promises. He promised the land to Abraham and his descendants, he promised to declare his people righteous if they believed in him, and he promised to rescue them from slavery. From Genesis to Joshua, we see a clear picture of God keeping his word and intervening on behalf of his people.

Everything God says has purpose. He doesn't make arbitrary decisions, and he doesn't sit idle while we figure out life alone. He sees each of our days, the path we are one, and where we need to go. He is faithful, and he fulfills every single promise he makes. We can trust him because he has proven himself worthy.

Lord, I trust in your promises today. You are faithful and worthy of everything I have to give.

Scripture Reading: Joshua 22-24

Choose Obedience

"Be very careful to follow everything Moses wrote in the Book of Instruction. Do not deviate from it, turning either to the right or to the left."

JOSHUA 23:6 NLT

God's people are always called to obedience. Moses was instructed to follow God's commands, Joshua was given the same instruction, and we too are told to faithfully do what God says. It is a privilege to be invited into the same calling as men like Moses and Joshua. What an honor it is to be prompted to carefully follow everything God has commanded.

It is unwise to be flippant with God's Word. Flirting with things that are contrary to his holiness never results in the satisfaction we expect. It's foolish to compromise our standards and think it won't have an impact. He has prepared a path for each of us, and following it isn't always easy, but it is worth it. His burden is not heavy, and his instructions generate freedom. His commands are good and true.

Jesus, give me grace to follow you. Soften my heart and help me take your commands seriously.

Scripture Reading: Judges 1-3

God's People

After that generation died, another generation grew up who did not acknowledge the LORD or remember the mighty things he had done for Israel.

JUDGES 2:10 NIV

The first few books of Judges highlights what happens when a nation embraces disobedience. Israel did not obey the Lord's commands, and we see them experience the consequences of their own actions. We also see God continue to be faithful despite their many downfalls. Ultimately, reading Judges gives us clear picture of the desperate need for an eternal deliverer.

Israel's history can stir up hope within us. It's tempting to look at our culture and be discouraged by the way each generation seems to fall further from the will of God. We see patterns and tendencies that people couldn't imagine decades ago. We must remember that God is capable of redeeming us no matter how many generations go astray. His plans will not be ruined by the actions of disobedient people.

Lord, remind me of the bigger picture today! Keep me from being discouraged and help me remember that you are faithful to redeem your people.

Scripture Reading: Judges 4-6

Stopping the Cycle

The LORD looked at him and said, "Go in this strength of yours and save Israel from the hand of Midian. Have I not sent you?"

JUDGES 6:14 NASB

There is a cycle repeated in the book of Judges. A generation came up who did what was right in their own eyes. They suffered under the consequence of their sin, and they cried out to God for deliverance. God heard them and faithfully raised up a judge to rescue them.

God is still faithful to rescue us when we go astray. He doesn't want us to keep going back to our own way of doing things. Through Jesus, he has given us the power to say no to our sinful patterns and embrace freedom and new life. We don't have to stay in a cycle of shame and fear. Christ is our judge and our deliverer. He is the final answer to our cry for help.

Jesus, free me from myself. May I accept you as my once-for-all Savior!

Scripture Reading: Judges 7-9

Don't Forget

The people of Israel did not remember the LORD their God, who had delivered them from the hand of all their enemies on every side, and they did not show steadfast love to the family of Jerubbaal (that is, Gideon) in return for all the good that he had done to Israel.

JUDGES 8:34-35 ESV

At last, the Israelites entered the land God had promised to Abraham, Isaac, and Jacob! They arrived after suffering for hundreds of years in slavery and forty years in the desert. They had reached the Promised Land, yet they quickly forgot God's faithfulness. They quickly surrendered themselves to other Gods, fleshly pleasures, and selfish pursuits.

How often do we behave just like the Israelites? We rejoice in the blessings God has showered upon us, and we quickly forget his goodness. Our attention spans are short, and our devotion isn't always steadfast. Let us remember the mighty things God has done! Let us strive to be a people who cling to the Lord and do not forget every big and small way he has intervened on our behalf.

Lord, help me pay attention to my commitment to you today. Don't let me fall away.

Scripture Reading: Judges 10-12

Prone to Wander

Then the Israelites put aside their foreign gods and served the Lord. And he was grieved by their misery.

Judges 10:16 NLT

The people of God are prone to wander. This has been a primary point in story of humanity up to this point in Scripture. Unfortunately, it will continue to be a primary point through the entirety of the Old Testament. We constantly see God calling his people back to him. He speaks through prophets and leaders, he warns his followers to stay faithful, and he grieves as they walk away from him.

God never gives up. He never stops pursuing his loved ones. He continues to make a way for us to be near him. Finally, through Christ, he provides the ultimate avenue for redemption. He clears the way so that nothing will stand in the way of communion with his people. Even though we wander, God invites us back time and time again. Even though our unfaithfulness grieves him, he mercifully gives us the gift of eternal life.

Lord, don't let me wander today. I am sorry for the grief that my wayward heart has caused you. Thank you for calling me back to you again and again.

Scripture Reading: Judges 13-15

Samson's Paradox

The Spirit of the LORD came powerfully upon him so that he tore the lion apart with his bare hands as he might have torn a young goat. But he told neither his father nor his mother what he had done.

JUDGES 14:6 NIV

This verse highlights the paradox of Samson. He is gifted to overcome opposition, yet he is also immature in the face of responsibility. Samson overwhelmed a lion that suddenly attacked him as he and his parents traveled to the city of Timnah. The Spirit of the Lord came powerfully on Samson, and he used his extraordinary strength to rip the lion apart.

Scripture emphasizes that he didn't tell his parents anything about this incident. This final note is important because Samson's carelessness kept his parents ignorant about the lion carcass. That very carcass would later cause him to break his Nazarite vow by scooping honey from it. This made his parents ritually unclean without their knowledge. The violation of his vow was a foreboding example of the complacency that later caused irreparable damage.

Lord, don't let me become complacent about the calling and skills you have given me.

Scripture Reading: Judges 16-18

Steadfast Love

"LORD God, please remember me. Strengthen me, God, just once more. With one act of vengeance, let me pay back the Philistines for my two eyes."

JUDGES 16:28 CSB

Throughout the Bible we read that the Lord is gracious and compassionate. He is slow to anger, and he is abounding in steadfast love. These characteristics of God are evident in the life of Samson. God was patient with him even though he gave him plenty of reasons to be angry. God gave him great talent and potential, yet Samson disregarded his responsibilities and flagrantly violated his vow to God.

At the end of his life, Samson finally prayed. It might not be a prayer that ends up on motivational posters, but it is a heart-felt prayer erupting from someone who became poor in spirit. He deeply regretted what he had done, and he poured his heart out to the Lord. God, in his steadfast love for both Samson and the people of Israel, heard Samson's cry. He met Samson's pleas with steadfast love even when he had every right to be angry.

God, thank you for patiently waiting for me when I choose the wrong path. Thank you for kindly leading me back to you every time.

Scripture Reading: Judges 19-21

The Final Word

In those days Israel had no king; all the people did whatever seemed right in their own eyes.
JUDGES 21:25 NLT

Today's Scripture is the final word on a series of alarming stories. The repetition of violence and sin in the book of Judges is indicative of what happens when people begin to judge what is right in their own eyes rather than trusting God's commands. When the moral standard for each person becomes "what looks good to me," people end up scrambling for their own gain at the expense of others.

Even more disturbing, perhaps, is the statement that Israel had no king. This sad commentary reveals that Israel had rejected God as their king. They had forgotten the God of their father Abraham. They had spurned the one true God who had rescued them from slavery in Egypt and shepherded them to the Promised Land. As a result, the people of Israel became rudderless. Israel's wandering in the desert may have ended hundreds of years before, but they were now wandering in the wilderness of their wayward sin.

Oh Lord, why would I trust myself to be the ruler of my life more than you? You are unfailing and full of love. Help me lean on you for my moral clarity today!

Scripture Reading: Ruth 1-4

A Faithful Life

"May the LORD repay you for what you have done. May you be richly rewarded by the LORD, the God of Israel, under whose wings you have come to take refuge."

RUTH 2:12 NIV

If we think about the men of the Bible whose character we want to emulate, we might overlook Boaz. He's not the most flashy, and his story isn't lengthy. If we take the time to learn about his life, we will find that he reflected many character traits of God. He was compassionate, successful, generous, and responsible. His care for Namoi and Ruth is admirable, and his commitment to honoring the Lord is worth noting.

Let's not forget the quiet and steady followers of God. Walking in the way of Christ isn't always loud or even noticeable. A steady commitment matters more than grandiose behavior. A heart that is devoted to God and his ways matters more than a sacrifice that everyone applauds. Service to others and consistency of character are the benchmarks for a life of faithfulness.

Lord, help me reflect the characteristics of manhood that are evident in the life of Boaz. Teach me how to be steady and consistent.

Scripture Reading: 1 Samuel 1-3

Posture of Prayer

The LORD came and stood, calling as at other times, "Samuel! Samuel!" And Samuel said, "Speak, for your servant hears."

1 SAMUEL 3:10 ESV

From his childhood onward, Samuel's life was marked by a posture of listening to God in prayer. As a small boy, in the quietness of the night, he heard God calling his name, and he responded with attentiveness. Later in life he became attuned to God's direction and learned to speak the word of God with confidence. He became adept at hearing God's voice and discerning his will in pivotal moments.

It's never too late to develop a posture of attentiveness toward God. It might not feel natural at first, but taking time to listen for God's voice is always fruitful. He doesn't always answer according to our own expectations, but he is faithful to speak to his people. He invites us to know him and be known by him in every season of life.

God, please speak to me and call me to respond to your work in my life. Give me discernment to know your voice and follow your will.

Scripture Reading: 1 Samuel 4-6

Disobedience and Compromise

That same day, a Benjaminite man ran from the battle and came to Shiloh. His clothes were torn, and there was dirt on his head.

1 SAMUEL 4:12 CSB

Eli served as the high priest of Israel for forty years. Sometimes he served faithfully, and sometimes he did not. In his good moments, he attentively cared for God's people. He prayed for Hannah, and he encouraged Samuel to respond to God's voice. In his moments of disobedience, he allowed sin to run rampant. He turned a blind eye to the atrocities committed by his sons who were supposed to represent God as priests of Israel.

Eventually, God's judgment caught up to Samuel and his sons. When the Ark of the Covenant was captured by the Philistines, Hophni and Phinehas were killed in the process. A horrified Benjamite man ran from the battle to tell the anxious high priest. This news overwhelmed Eli, and he fell backward off his chair and broke his neck. His disobedience and compromise were his downfall.

Lord, let me serve you faithfully for all the days of my life. Help me choose integrity even when it's uncomfortable or seemingly insignificant.

Scripture Reading: 1 Samuel 7-9

Raising an Ebenezer

Samuel then took a large stone and placed it between the towns of Mizpah and Jeshanah. He named it Ebenezer (which means "the stone of help"), for he said, "Up to this point the LORD has helped us!"

1 SAMUEL 7:12 NLT

Sometimes we skim past words in Scripture that aren't easily understood. We overlook them in favor of finishing our reading plan instead of pausing to take in their depth. This could be true with today's reading. We've heard the word *ebenezer*, but maybe we haven't taken the time to understand what it means.

The word *ebenezer* has its roots in 1 Samuel. In the face of a vast Philistine army, the prophet Samuel urged the people of Israel to turn their hearts to the Lord and pray for rescue. As their enemy gathered to attack, the Lord spoke with a thunderous voice from heaven which panicked the enemy and gave Israel the victory. Afterward, Samuel built a memorial that he intentionally named "Ebenezer" so that future generations could remember how the Lord had helped his people.

Lord, I praise you for all you have done to help me throughout my life. Today, let me continue to come to you for help.

Scripture Reading: 1 Samuel 10-12

Serve God Alone

"Only fear the LORD and serve Him in truth with all your heart; for consider what great things He has done for you."
1 SAMUEL 12:24 NASB

Samuel daily lived out the words of this verse for his entire life. He served God with reverence and respect even when cultural trends and powerful leaders discouraged him to do so. He had seen God do so much for both himself and Israel that he couldn't imagine walking away from his relationship with the Lord.

Samuel wanted others to experience God's faithfulness. He wanted them to take notice of the great things God had done. He was concerned that the people were being swept away into sinful thinking as the influential people in their society flirted with other gods and other systems of morality. Samuel longed for the Israelites to make God the priority of their lives. He wanted them to worship God with all their heart and avoid worshipping worthless things.

God, how could I not fear you and serve you every day? You have been so faithful and kind to me.

Scripture Reading: 1 Samuel 13-15

Immutable

"He who is the Glory of Israel does not lie or change his mind; for he is not a human being, that he should change his mind."

1 Samuel 15:29 niv

In today's reading, King Saul, who had changed allegiance between the Lord and pagan gods several times over the years, pleaded once again for mercy. Samuel pointed out to him that Saul's vacillating commitments did not reflect God's image. God's perspective was completely consistent. God does not change his mind or waver in thought. He is steady and reliable in all things.

God is immutable. This means that he does not change. There is no lack of knowledge, ability, or comprehension in God. He is transcendent. He created time and, therefore, is not confined to the laws of time. He created the world and, therefore, is not subject to the laws of the world. He created humans and, therefore, is not dependent upon the whims of human experience.

Lord, forgive me for my easily wavering mind. Please shape my thoughts to consistently reflect your righteousness and will for my life.

Scripture Reading: 1 Samuel 16-18

Look on the Heart

"Do not look on his appearance or on the height of his stature, because I have rejected him. For the LORD sees not as man sees: man looks on the outward appearance, but the LORD looks on the heart."

1 SAMUEL 16:7 ESV

Even Samuel made the mistake of judging the sons of Jesse on first impressions. He had been commissioned by God to choose a new king for Israel. At first glance, it seemed to Samuel that Eliab fit the look of a king. God challenged Samuel to not judge the anointed one based on his appearance, height, or stature. God wanted Samuel to look deeper at the heart of the individual God had selected.

This set a precedence that God would be faithful to throughout history. He consistently calls people who don't fit our human standards. He is not discouraged by our weaknesses, and he is not impressed by the things we think are brag worthy. He cares so much more about what is in our hearts. His instruction to Samuel reminds us that his perspective is far more important than what we see with our earthly eyes.

Lord, I am often guilty of overlooking those who are not outwardly impressive. Help me see with your eyes.

Scripture Reading: 1 Samuel 19-21

An Unbreakable Bond

"Go in peace, for we have sworn loyalty to each other in the LORD's name. The LORD is the witness of a bond between us and our children forever." Then David left, and Jonathan returned to the town.

1 SAMUEL 20:42 NLT

David, who had been anointed the future king of Israel, was being hunted by Saul. Jonathan, the son of Saul and the prince of Israel, remained loyal to his trusted friend David. He did not waver even as his own Dad breathed threats against them both. David and Jonathan were not going to let King Saul's instability derail their friendship. Their bond of friendship was deeper than any hostility.

We can pretend to be strong on our own, but the truth is that we need the support of brotherhood. We need men of integrity to call us to a higher standard, and we need men who are kind to listen and give advice. We need men who are faithful to encourage us in our walk with the Lord, and we need men who are loyal to stand with us when life is filled with trials.

God, bring men into my life that show the loyalty that David and Jonathan shared. Thank you for the gift of brotherhood.

Scripture Reading: 1 Samuel 22-24

David's Confidence

"May the Lord be judge and decide between you and me. May he take notice and plead my case and deliver me from you."

1 Samuel 24:15 CSB

David could have seized power for himself by killing Saul. After all, King Saul certainly had been trying to kill David. In the eyes of the world, David was more than justified to act with violence against the unstable, hostile king of Israel. However, David chose to trust God's plan instead. He decided he didn't need to take matters into his own hands because the circumstances were already in God's hands.

While Saul struggled with anxiety attacks and deteriorating mental health, David found stability in his relationship with God. David knew that God was faithful and just, and he knew that God's long-range plan would not be thwarted by short-term events. David leaned on the Lord and trusted him for the outcome. He confidently honored God even while Saul breathed threats of evil.

Lord, may my actions today reflect the confidence I have in you.

Scripture Reading: 1 Samuel 25-27

Trusted Men

Then David said to Ahimelech the Hittite and to Abishai the son of Zeruiah, Joab's brother, saying, "Who will go down with me to Saul in the camp?" And Abishai said, "I will go down with you."

1 Samuel 26:6 NASB

David had some trusted friends and confidants. He could rely on them to stand by him through the most difficult of tasks. In today's reading David had a particularly dangerous mission ahead, and he needed a wing man. He knew he could trust Ahimelech and Abishai for the job. Abishai volunteered first and set off with David.

Every man needs an Ahimelech and Abishai in their life. Every man needs trusted friends, tested through the seasons of life, who will show up in times of need. In today's world, these are the men who don't hesitate to help when called. They move furniture, change tires, celebrate achievements, and help solve problems. They confront poor behavior, are resilient through suffering, and remain steadfast through disappointment.

Lord, thank you for the men in my life who have my back. Please deepen these commitments and encourage me to lean on them for help.

Scripture Reading: 1 Samuel 28-31

Generating Unity

David replied, "No, my brothers, you must not do that with what the LORD has given us. He has protected us and delivered into our hands the raiding party that came against us."

1 SAMUEL 30:23 NIV

Some of David's men had become too exhausted to continue fighting. David ordered them to stay behind to guard the equipment as the rest of his men went on to fight. After the victory, some of the fighting men demanded that those who stayed behind be penalized. They declared that the spoils of the battle should not be shared with those who didn't fight.

David urged them to get rid of selfish attitudes. Self-promotion at the expense of putting others down would create long-lasting strife. He modeled a posture that generated unity and benefited the community as a whole. He knew that when people think of themselves as better than others, division, hostility, and judgment are the outcomes. When people consider others before themselves, unity, generosity, and celebration are produced.

Lord, may my life be marked by unselfish gratitude for all you have provided and may I be generous as a result today.

Scripture Reading: 2 Samuel 1-3

King of Judah

The men of Judah came to David and anointed him king over the people of Judah.

2 Samuel 2:4 NLT

The moment when the men of Judah recognize David as their king is a significant milestone in biblical history. David was an ancestor of Judah, the father of the tribe and territory where these men now reside. When Judah had been alive, his father, Jacob, had prophesied that Israel's future king would be from the line of Judah. Now, in this moment, the promised royal line was officially recognized by the people.

Part of the royal prophecy over Judah and David also included reference to an eternal Messiah, the Lion of Judah, whose throne would last forever. The Bible stresses that the Messiah would be born in Bethlehem as David had been, would be a shepherd as David had been, and be anointed the everlasting King of Kings. With this moment, the prophecies of the coming King grow one step closer to completion.

Jesus, I see your story woven throughout the pages of Scripture. You are the King of Kings and Lord of Lords. I will worship and serve you today.

Scripture Reading: 2 Samuel 4-6

Foolish for God

"Yes, and I am willing to look even more foolish than this, even to be humiliated in my own eyes! But those servant girls you mentioned will indeed think I am distinguished!"

2 Samuel 6:22 NLT

No one could call David a stuffy, reserved worshipper. He followed the liturgy and engaged in the regular rhythms of the worshipping community, but no one could say that David was stuck in rote routines of religion. No, even in the grand regulations of Israel's religious system, David's expression of faith was fresh, raw, and unbridled. He danced in joy before the Lord and was unashamed despite his position as the king of Israel.

His wife, Michal, was embarrassed by David's outpouring of love toward God. She was disgusted by his undignified behavior. She thought he looked foolish, and she worried about what others would think. David's reply is a reminder that it is better look foolish to others because of our love for God than to dampen our relationship with God to look wise in this world.

Lord, I want to be close to you more than I want to perform for the expectations of others.

April

The revelation of your word brings light
and gives understanding to the
inexperienced.

Psalm 119:130 CSB

Scripture Reading: 2 Samuel 7-9

Eternal Lineage

"When your days are fulfilled and you lie down with your fathers, I will raise up your offspring after you, who shall come from your body, and I will establish his kingdom."

2 Samuel 7:12 esv

Nathan the prophet described to David how God had taken him from tending sheep in the pasture to tending God's people Israel. Nathan reminded David that he had been selected by God to be anointed king, and he promised that David's name would become famous throughout the earth. He promised that one of David's descendants would build a home for God and that God would establish his throne there forever.

One thousand years after Nathan's prophecy, the apostle Peter stood before a great crowd and proclaimed that Jesus, the descendant of David, was the King whose reign would last forever. Through Christ, God established his throne on earth. His death and resurrection created a way for all people to dwell with him forever.

Jesus, you are my King, and you have given my life to you. Thank you for your salvation. Help me share this good news with others today.

Scripture Reading: 2 Samuel 10-12

Guilty Party

Then Nathan said to David, "You are the man! This is what the LORD, the God of Israel, says: 'I anointed you king over Israel, and I delivered you from the hand of Saul.'"

2 SAMUEL 12:7 NIV

David, a man after God's own heart, who had walked so closely with the Lord and worshipped so freely throughout his lifetime, sinned terribly. He committed adultery with Bathsheba, and he arranged the murder of Bathsheba's husband. He tried to cover up these sins by involving others in his wickedness.

Nathan the prophet was fully aware of David's guilt. He told David a story about a wealthy man with a huge flock of sheep who stole a poor man's only sheep and slaughtered it for a dinner party. David was incensed at the audacity of this wealthy man! How could such a thing happen in his kingdom? David demanded to know who could have done such a terrible thing so that he could execute judgment. He was so wrapped up in his own desires that he couldn't see his situation clearly.

Lord, may I never become so blind in my laziness and arrogance that I fail to recognize the sin I have committed.

Scripture Reading: 2 Samuel 13-15

Promise of Power

Absalom did this with everyone who came to the king for judgment, and so he stole the hearts of all the people of Israel.

2 SAMUEL 15:6 NLT

Absalom didn't like the way his father, David, was leading the kingdom any longer. In fact, he thought that he would be a better leader than his dad. So, Absalom began sowing seeds of discontent throughout the kingdom. He'd shower affection on the crowds while painting his father as disconnected and uncaring. Absalom was manipulative, and he took advantage of his position to undermine David's leadership. He twisted conversations and inserted distrust for God's appointed ruler.

How we conduct ourselves from the second chair reveals a lot about our character. Our ability to remain humble, kind, and servant hearted under the promise of power and promotion is eye opening. It is important to consider the words we speak about those in authority and the motivations we have for caring for others.

Lord, don't let me be like Absalom who schemed for personal gain by undercutting the leaders above him.

Scripture Reading: 2 Samuel 16-18

Taking Our Place

Then the king trembled and went up to the chamber over the gate and wept. And this is what he said as he walked: "My son Absalom, my son, my son Absalom! If only I had died instead of you, Absalom, my son, my son!"

2 Samuel 18:33 NASB

David mourned the loss of his son even though Absalom was destructive and rebellious. He had never dreamed of a life where his own son would violently betray him and end up being killed in his insurrection. No father wants to lose relationship with their child, so David grieved. He agonized for his son. He mourned Absalom's suffering with anger. He longed to be able to take his son's place.

It is this sentiment that led Jesus to voluntarily give up his life on the cross for the sins of the world. God's children had gotten caught up in their rebellion. They had betrayed God's authority and revolted. Their sin was leading them to a terrible death, so Jesus stepped in and took the place of those who had sinned against God. He changed the course of history even though we've done nothing to deserve it.

Jesus, thank you for agonizing over me. Thank you for rescuing me from my own rebellious heart. Thank you for taking my place in death. I will live for you today!

Scripture Reading: 2 Samuel 19-21

Forgiveness

Then, turning to Shimei, David vowed,
"Your life will be spared."
2 Samuel 19:23 NLT

Shimei was a Benjamite who cursed David during Absalom's rebellion. When David returned to the throne, Shimei sought forgiveness. Shimei had done horrible things to David, and it would have made perfect sense for David to hold it against him. Given the opportunity, David could have sought vengeance or held a grudge. Instead, he chose to spare Shimei's life and show mercy.

We don't always have the chance to formally extend forgiveness. Sometimes the people who hurt us don't admit they were wrong. When that happens, we lean on the strength of the Holy Spirit to heal and choose forgiveness anyway. When someone does express their sorrow for what they've done, we have a beautiful opportunity to speak kindly and choose mercy in a tangible way.

Lord, give me the strength I need to forgive even when I don't want to. Help me respond to the people who've hurt me with mercy and kindness.

Scripture Reading: 2 Samuel 22-24

Pause to Praise

"Who is God, but the Lord?
And who is a rock, except our God?
This God is my strong refuge
and has made my way blameless."
2 Samuel 22:32-33 esv

As David looked back on the victories God had provided, he couldn't help but praise him. He unleashed his creative talent and wrote a long, dynamic psalm that told the story of God's powerful work, trustworthy commands, and faithful protection. This psalm offers unbridled praise to God as David remembers specifically how God rescued him from his enemies. It tells of David's dependency on God for continued help, and it declares his resilient commitment to the Lord.

We all have instances of God's faithful provision. We each have a unique story. The details don't matter as much as our willingness to offer our story to God in worship. We can pay attention to how God has shown up for us, and we can declare his goodness despite our circumstances.

God, forgive me for going through life without stopping to articulate all that you have done for me. Help me pause today to acknowledge you as the rock and refuge of my life.

Scripture Reading: 1 Kings 1-3

Final Words

"I am going where everyone on earth must someday go. Take courage and be a man. Observe the requirements of the LORD your God, and follow all his ways. Keep the decrees, commands, regulations, and laws written in the Law of Moses so that you will be successful in all you do and wherever you go."

1 KINGS 2:2-3 NLT

As David's death approached, he wanted to leave his son Solomon with some wise parting words. He offered the sobering recognition that he was about to die, and he was honest with Solomon about his final days. He encouraged his son to be brave even though he knew he was on his way to the grave.

David urged Solomon to follow God's ways and keep his commands. He wanted to leave Solomon with the reminder that a man's true success occurs when that man obeys God. His legacy was one of following hard after God. Nothing else was as important as that one priority.

Heavenly Father, let me speak as audaciously and clearly about life as David does to his son. Help my mind be focused and my heart sincere.

Scripture Reading: 1 Kings 4-6

Unrivaled Wisdom

He was wiser than anyone—wiser than Ethan the Ezrahite, and Heman, Calcol, and Darda, sons of Mahol. His reputation extended to all the surrounding nations.

1 Kings 4:31 CSB

God had gifted Solomon with unrivaled wisdom. The Bible describes Solomon's wisdom as exceeding all the wise men of the East and Egypt. He was wiser than some of the greatest thinkers Israel had seen. Solomon's reputation spread through the surrounding nations. They would send delegates to learn from him and marvel at his accomplishments.

Despite his wisdom Solomon allowed himself to be captured in the trappings of his own splendor. The accumulation of wealth, wives, and weapons of warfare eventually tricked him into complacency in his walk with God, proving that no one's mind is immune to manipulation and temptation.

Lord, I am not as wise as Solomon. If he could fall into temptation over the course of his life, I could easily as well. Protect me from the trappings of this world.

Scripture Reading: 1 Kings 7-9

Commissioning

"May he turn our hearts to him, to walk in obedience to him and keep the commands, decrees and laws he gave our ancestors."

1 KINGS 8:58 NIV

The temple was a grand architectural marvel, but the true awe-inspiring value of this new building was not found in its grandiose size, mountain-top location, impressive gold overlays, or sacred artifacts included within. The true significance of this building was that the temple was God's home on earth. It was a place where the Lord would rest his presence among his people.

Solomon delivered a prayer of commissioning at the dedication of the temple. His prayer expresses awe at the fact that God could dwell with people. He felt wonder at the fact that God, who could not be contained by the heavens, would constrain himself to a location on the earth. He realized that God would choose to be with his people because he loved them. He was astonished by God's willingness to be near his creation.

Lord, your willingness to dwell among us demonstrates how much you love us. Be with me by your Spirit and help me live in obedience to you.

Scripture Reading: 1 Kings 10-12

Stay Pure

He had 700 wives, who were princesses, and 300 concubines. And his wives turned away his heart.

1 Kings 11:3 ESV

Solomon had been told not to marry multiple women. He had been clearly instructed by the Lord to not marry women from other nations who followed other gods. He was warned that his heart would be led away from his commitment to the Lord and turned toward other gods. Solomon knew the potential fruit of his disobedience, and he followed his own desires anyway.

How can we avoid the pitfalls of sin? We must daily choose obedience to God. The destruction of our own bad choices is not a mystery. Scripture is filled with encouragement to heed God's commands and follow his ways. As we stay rooted in truth and grounded in the Word, God offers us protection from temptation. He gives us all the tools we need to say no to the desires of our flesh.

God, lead me not into temptation but deliver me from evil, for yours is the kingdom and the glory and the power forever and ever.

Scripture Reading: 1 Kings 13-15

Resilient King

Asa did what was pleasing in the Lord's sight, as his ancestor David had done.

1 Kings 15:11 NLT

A back-and-forth pattern emerges in the historical books of 1 & 2 Kings and 1 & 2 Chronicles. In these books, Israel and Judah become ground zero for a cosmic battle. Many of the kings choose to do what is evil in the eyes of God, but some of the kings choose to do what is pleasing in the Lord's sight. This cycle repeats itself again and again for generations until the Lord finally puts an end to it and scatters his people in exile.

Here, in today's reading, the pattern has taken root. King Jeroboam of the northern tribes rejected God to the point of making golden calves to worship. King Rehoboam of Judah also did evil in the Lord's sight. King Abijam, Rehoboam's son, committed the same sins as his father, but King Asa of Judah refreshingly decided to do what was pleasing in the Lord's sight. He followed the example of his ancestor David. Asa removed the pagan shrines and remained completely faithful to the Lord throughout his life.

Lord, help me be resilient in the face of evil. Help me do what is pleasing in your sight despite what is culturally popular.

Scripture Reading: 1 Kings 16-18

Proven Faithful

"How long are you going to struggle with the two choices? If the LORD is God, follow Him; but if Baal, follow him." But the people did not answer him so much as a word.

1 KINGS 18:21 NASB

The scene in today's reading is dramatic. Nearly a thousand servants of the false gods Baal and Asherah were wailing and thrashing themselves trying to get the attention of their deity. Elijah mocked their efforts as they stayed committed to their idol worship. The false prophets cut themselves and screamed, but they received no reply. When Elijah asked God to intervene, he faithfully revealed his power and glory.

We are called to follow the one true God even if the crowd is moving in another direction. We are called to remain steadfast even if the loudest voices clamor for influence and captivate the attention of the masses. God remains steady despite the shaking of the earth. He remains strong despite the chaos that seems to be thriving. We can trust him because his truth will remain above all else.

Lord, give me the courage to stand firmly in your truth.

Scripture Reading: 1 Kings 19-22

In the Quiet

When Elijah heard it, he pulled his cloak over his face and went out and stood at the mouth of the cave. Then a voice said to him, "What are you doing here, Elijah?"

1 Kings 19:13 NIV

Even Elijah grew faint of heart. He was considered to be a great prophet, and he still experienced common human weakness. In today's Scripture he led one of the most dramatic spiritual encounters the world had ever witnessed. He stood by himself against false prophets, and he won. Jezebel's anger raged, and she issued an execution order against Elijah. He ran for forty days and nights all the way to Mount Sinai where he hid in a cave.

God showed up while Elijah hid. He asked him what he was doing, and Elijah sheepishly confessed that he felt alone and was scared. In response, the Lord instructed Elijah to stand outside the cave while he passed by. As Elijah stood, a mighty windstorm, earthquake, and then a fire rattled the mountain. The Lord was not in any of these, but after all the commotion the Lord drew near to Elijah with a gentle whisper.

God, I am here seeking you today because I need you and I want you to live through me. Help me listen attentively to your still, small voice.

Scripture Reading: 2 Kings 1-3

Embrace Opportunities

He took up the cloak of Elijah that had fallen from him and went back and stood on the bank of the Jordan.

2 Kings 2:13 ESV

Elisha adored his older mentor, Elijah. He watched for years as Elijah resisted the threats and wickedness of evil kings. He had seen Elijah walk through a wayward culture with deep resiliency of faith and unwavering integrity. He had seen Elijah do great, miraculous things for God. After his hero had been taken away into glory, Elisha had a decision to make. Would he be bold enough to carry on the important calling that Elijah had carried so well for so long? Would he be willing to pick up Elijah's burden and continue the good work with as much focus and determination?

Elisha inherited quite a legacy from Elijah, but he had to decide what he was going to do with it. Many of us will face similar situations in our lifetimes. We might be presented with opportunities or privileges, but we are each responsible for how we handle them. Will we embrace the path God puts in front of us, or will we turn away from his provision?

Lord, help me embrace the opportunities you put in front of me. Give me the courage I need to walk the way you would have me go.

Scripture Reading: 2 Kings 4-6

Open Our Eyes

"O Lord, open his eyes and let him see!" The Lord opened the young man's eyes, and when he looked up, he saw that the hillside around Elisha was filled with horses and chariots of fire.

2 Kings 6:17 NLT

We can't see everything that the Lord is doing. Our perspective is limited, and we have difficulty understanding what he is doing behind the scenes. Our ability to recognize his activity doesn't determine its existence. He is always moving and working everything together for his glory and our good.

Elisha wants his servant to understand this truth. He wants him to know that God operates in a way that goes beyond our comprehension. The battles God fights are not simply against rulers of this world who exist in flesh and blood. God engages in an ancient battle against the powers and principalities of spiritual darkness and evil. He is at work in unseen ways to bring about the restoration of all things.

Lord, open my eyes to see that you are actively working in ways I cannot understand. I trust you as you work in my own life today.

Scripture Reading: 2 Kings 7-9

Commissioned for Cleansing

They quickly took their cloaks and spread them under him on the bare steps. Then they blew the trumpet and shouted, "Jehu is king!"

2 Kings 9:13 NIV

In today's Scripture Elisha summoned a young prophet to find a man named Jehu. Elisha instructed him to call Jehu into a private meeting and then to anoint Jehu as the next king of the northern tribes of Israel. Elisha suggested that as soon as the task was completed, he should run for his life. When Jehu shared what had happened with his fellow officers, they spread their cloaks before him so that Jehu wouldn't have to touch the ground. Then they celebrated and proclaimed him their new king, commissioning him to rid the land of religious sin that had compromised the land.

We see this mirrored in the life of Christ. When Jesus entered Jerusalem the people welcomed him as their king, and they spread their cloaks on the ground as Jesus passed by. Jesus immediately went into the temple and drove out the religious sin that had compromised God's house.

Jesus, all that I have is yours, and I lay it before you. You are my king. I will serve you with my life.

Scripture Reading: 2 Kings 10-12

A Refreshing Reprieve

Throughout the time the priest Jehoiada instructed him,
Joash did what was right in the LORD's sight.

2 KINGS 12:2 CSB

The political upheaval of these historical books can be difficult for modern readers to follow. The nation of Israel broke into two kingdoms after Solomon's reign. The larger northern kingdom retained the name of Israel, and the southern kingdom became known as Judah. Kings came and went over many generations. Some would be faithful to God, but sadly most were not. Eventually the corruption of the rulers and the adulterous behavior of the citizens led God to allow both nations to be conquered.

As readers study these chapters in 2 Kings, it is refreshing to find a moment of reprieve from the depravity. In today's reading we see a wise priest named Jehoiada and a young king named Joash stand in contrast to the trends of their culture. They did what was right in the eyes of the Lord despite a historic tendency to fail at honoring him.

Lord, help me stand in contrast to those around me who refuse to follow you. May I encourage others to be faithful to your ways.

Scripture Reading: 2 Kings 13-15

Relatively Speaking

He did what was right in the sight of the LORD, yet not like his father David; he acted in accordance with everything that his father Joash had done.

2 KINGS 14:3 NASB

Relatively speaking Amaziah was a good king. He stood out compared to the many evil kings that had taken the throne in Judah over the generations. He did a good job of following God's commands, but like his father Joash Amaziah also failed to remove the pagan shrines where the people of Judah were offering sacrifices and prayers.

The Bible notes that these two relatively good kings were compromised in their faith. While they themselves did what was right in God's sight, they were not personally devoted to him the way their ancestor David had been. This is a good reminder to us to not measure our spiritual worth against the standard of others around us. The measurement of how we are doing in our walk of faith rests purely in the eyes of God.

Lord, let me walk without compromise in my commitments today.

Scripture Reading: 2 Kings 16-18

Don't Be Stubborn

The Israelites would not listen. They were as stubborn as their ancestors who had refused to believe in the LORD their God.

2 KINGS 17:14 NLT

Even as the kingdom of Israel crumbled, the people refused to return to the Lord. God sent prophet after prophet to call them back to faithfulness. He gave the warning after warning to turn from worshipping idols and follow God's commands. The nation of Israel experienced the Lord's steadfast love for generations, and they still stubbornly chose the destruction of their faith.

Israel's destruction came in many forms. They worshipped other Gods, did things in secret, copied the ways of surrounding nations, rejected God's standards, and sold themselves to evil. They followed the path of fulfilling their selfish desires and looking for earthly gain over eternal promises. We can learn from their example and humbly ask God to examine our lives. Our willingness to open our hearts to him will dictate the strength or weakness of our faith.

Lord, it is hard to believe a nation could wander so far from your ways. Please step in and keep me on the right path. May my thoughts, words, and actions be honoring to you.

Scripture Reading: 2 Kings 19-20

Prayer of Deliverance

"LORD our God, deliver us from his hand, so that all the kingdoms of the earth may know that you alone, LORD, are God."

2 KINGS 19:19 NIV

The people of Judah woke up from a spiritual stupor. They watched the decimation of the northern tribes at the hands of Assyria, and they realized they needed to repent and be right with the Lord. So, when King Hezekiah ascended to the throne in Jerusalem, he and the people cleansed the land of pagan shrines. Hezekiah and his people remained faithful to the Lord and obeyed the commands God had given Moses.

As the foreign nations threatened Judah, Hezekiah sought the Lord for help. The Prophet Isaiah relayed a message of deliverance to Judah because of Hezekiah's trust in the Lord. No nation would be able to conquer them as long as they remained faithful to the Lord.

God, thank you for the prayer of Hezekiah. May I stop the flow of my life often to lift up my concerns to you and ask you for protection.

Scripture Reading: 2 Kings 21-23

The Best Response

The king went up to the house of the LORD.... And he read in their hearing all the words of the Book of the Covenant that had been found in the house of the LORD.

2 KINGS 23:2 ESV

The rediscovery of God's Word sparked a renewal of faith among the people of Judah. It seems the general population had lost knowledge of God's Word. They had become biblically illiterate, but the truth was revealed when Hilkiah rediscovered the ancient manuscript of the Book of the Law. He was the high priest who served in the temple, and he began to read the book to Josiah the king of Judah.

Upon hearing the words written in the Book of the Law, Josiah tore his clothes and repented to God. The living and active Word of God had cut to the core of his soul. Josiah fell before the Lord and begged for forgiveness and mercy. The king then had the entire Book of the Law read for the people of Judah and launched waves of revival throughout the land.

Lord, let me never lose sight of your Word. Bring our land back to an understanding of the Bible and change our hearts toward you.

Scripture Reading: 2 Kings 24-25

Still True

All the people from the least to the greatest, together with the army officers, fled to Egypt for fear of the Babylonians.
2 Kings 25:26 NIV

Nearly a thousand years prior to today's Scripture God had orchestrated the greatest rescue mission in history. The Exodus of God's people from slavery in Egypt was a miraculous testimony of his goodness, but now the people were desperately fleeing back to the land where they were held captive. Their situation had become so dire that they saw fleeing the Promised Land for their previous land of enslavement as the best course of action.

How could this have happened? How could God's own special people have fallen so far that they were conquered by other nations and scattered as war-torn refugees across the globe? What about the promises of God to Abraham and Moses? What about the unending royal line of King David? What about the promised Messiah who was going to bless the entire world from his throne in Jerusalem?

Heavenly Father, let me lean into the misery of this verse and learn to trust your overarching plan of salvation.

Scripture Reading: 1 Chronicles 1-3

Knowing Their History

The sons of Abraham were Isaac and Ishmael.

1 Chronicles 1:28 NASB

The Old Testament frequently establishes the identity of the people of Israel. The genealogical record of God's people is significant to the story that unfolds throughout the pages of the Bible. So, 1 Chronicles begins with an ancestral record explaining the uniqueness of the nation of Israel.

Israel descended from Abraham and his son, Isaac. Isaac's son, Jacob, would have his name changed by God to Israel. From him would come an entire nation set apart to proclaim God's glory on earth and invite people into his blessing. This nation would become vast during its four hundred years of enslavement in Egypt and resolute in its forty years of wandering in the desert. This nation would struggle to establish itself in the land God had given to Abraham and struggle further as their kings plunged them into compromise and chaos. Knowing the story of Israel is important to understanding the salvation plan of God that would come in the generations ahead.

Jesus, help me better appreciate the history of your people through the Old Testament so that I might have a better grasp of your character and your story.

Scripture Reading: 1 Chronicles 4-6

An Inspirational Sidebar

"Oh, that you would bless me and expand my territory! Please be with me in all that I do, and keep me from all trouble and pain!" And God granted him his request.

1 Chronicles 4:10 NLT

Embedded in the historical book of 1 Chronicles is this brief description of a man named Jabez. No one else in this chapter is given more than a phrase of description, but Jabez is awarded several inspirational sentences. We learn that he was more honorable than any of his brothers. We learn that his mother, after a difficult childbirth, had given him a name that means distress or pain. Most importantly we learn that Jabez was the one who prayed for God's blessing.

Jabez asked God to expand what he had already entrusted to him. He prayed that God would be with him in all that he did. Jabez prayed that God would keep him from trouble and pain, and God heard his prayers. His story is an encouragement to us that we serve a God who is attentive to our cries.

Lord, may I seek you the way that Jabez did. May I ask for your blessing and may I keep my priorities true to you.

Scripture Reading: 1 Chronicles 7-9

Your Legacy

Shallum was the son of Kore, a descendant of Abiasaph, from the clan of Korah. He and his relatives, the Korahites, were responsible for guarding the entrance to the sanctuary, just as their ancestors had guarded the Tabernacle in the camp of the LORD.

1 CHRONICLES 9:19 NLT

Shallum's family had performed their responsibilities with faithfulness and effectiveness over generations. His job had been to guard the entrance of the sanctuary in Jerusalem after God's people returned from exile. Keeping watch over who was able to enter the temple had been the job of his ancestors for over a thousand years. Readers of 1 Chronicles get the sense that this small note contained deep significance in the storyline of God's faithfulness to Israel and the desire of God's people to be consistently faithful to him.

Many of us don't have jobs that span generations of dedication, but we do each have a calling that spans thousands of years. We, like Shallum and others before him, have been called to serve the Lord faithfully in whatever vocation he has given us. He sets a path before us, and we get to choose whether to honor him with our days or not.

Lord, let my legacy be one of long, faithful service to you.

Scripture Reading: 1 Chronicles 10-12

Exegeting Culture

Of Issachar, men who had understanding of the times, to know what Israel ought to do, 200 chiefs, and all their kinsmen under their command.

1 Chronicles 12:32 ESV

There were many talented people among David's committed leaders. In today's verse we read an interesting account of some of them. The men of Issachar understood the signs of the times and could discern the best course of action for Israel. These men could exegete culture. In other words, they could examine the layout of the society around them, interpret the meaning of the information they observed, and then implement a plan for the way forward.

Such a gift would be useful today. We need men who can look at the layout of the society around us through the lens of God, interpret what is happening in such a way that people can see the patterns, and then decipher the best way to be resilient and faithful. We need those who are equipped with the wisdom of God to speak up and lead in a way that honors the Lord.

God, increase my ability to discern what is happening in the culture around me and show me the best way through.

Scripture Reading: 1 Chronicles 13-15

Faithful and Strong

David and his troops went up to Baal-perazim and defeated the Philistines there. "God did it!" David exclaimed. "He used me to burst through my enemies like a raging flood!" So they named that place Baal-perazim (which means "the Lord who bursts through").

1 CHRONICLES 14:11 NLT

David's confidence came from his faith in God. He knew that he couldn't rely on his own talents or abilities. He was assured of victory and deliverance because he trusted God. He knew that the Lord, and anyone who was operating within the Lord's will, could burst through any barrier. As a result of his faith David's fame spread everywhere, and the Lord caused all the nations to fear him.

We all have obstacles in life. We face obstruction that seems insurmountable, but we must remember that nothing is impossible for the Lord. He doesn't fret over our trials or worry about our failures. As we establish a deeper level of trust in God, we will learn that his strength is more than enough for us. His strength is faithful, reliable, and better than any skill we could develop on our own.

Lord, break through the barriers in my faith and in my life. Help me trust your guidance and power to accomplish your will.

Scripture Reading: 1 Chronicles 16-18

Psalm of Praise

Give thanks to the LORD; call on his name;
proclaim his deeds among the peoples.
Sing to him; sing praise to him;
tell about all his wondrous works!

1 CHRONICLES 16:8-9 CSB

The song in the sixteenth chapter of 1 Chronicles is a combination of Psalm 105, 96, and 106 in that order. In contrast, it could be said that portions of those psalms are derived from today's Scripture. No matter which came first, certainly any scripture that quotes itself is worthy of special attention.

After the Ark of the Covenant had successfully been retrieved from the Philistines and relocated to its rightful place in Jerusalem, David gave his worship leaders a song of thanksgiving. The song lavished God with praise and proclaimed the wondrous works of God through the history of Israel. The song urged everyone on earth to recognize the Good News of salvation that God offered to the world. The song suggested that people should join in praise to God because even the trees and fields of creation were going to burst out in joy.

Lord, let my soul sing with joy today for all you have done in my life.

Scripture Reading: 1 Chronicles 19-21

Ultimate Mediator

David looked up and saw the angel of the LORD standing between heaven and earth with his sword drawn, reaching out over Jerusalem. So David and the leaders of Israel put on burlap to show their deep distress and fell face down on the ground.

1 CHRONICLES 21:16 NLT

David stood as a mediator between the angel of the Lord and the people of Jerusalem. He stood in the gap and took the blame for sin. He proclaimed the people were innocent and he urged the angel not to destroy them.

This moment happened in the very location that would become the site of the temple. It was the site where Abraham put his faith in God to provide a sacrifice in place of Isaac. It was a sacred place where God showed up and provided a mediator to offer forgiveness and take away the guilt of sin. Realizing this, David was overcome by the patience, mercy, and goodness of God.

Lord, thank you for your story salvation throughout the Bible. You have always mediated for us. Thank you for sending Jesus as the ultimate mediator of our salvation.

Scripture Reading: 1 Chronicles 22-24

Key to Success

"May the Lord give you discretion and understanding when he puts you in command over Israel, so that you may keep the law of the Lord your God."

1 Chronicles 22:12 NIV

The important question in David's mind was not whether Solomon would follow in his footsteps, but whether Solomon would follow the steps of God. He knew that in order for him to be successful he would need to carefully obey the decrees and regulations that the Lord gave to Israel. He wanted his son to seek the Lord with all his heart and soul.

What mattered to David most was Solomon's faith in the Lord. The opportunity to build the temple paled in comparison to David's desire that his son would walk in the ways of God. He knew that everything would fall into place if only Solomon would be uncompromised in his faith. He knew that the one thing that could tear down a kingdom was a king who was unfaithful in his love for God. Such a man couldn't expect God's blessing to continue unhindered.

God, help me be a man of uncompromised faith. None of my goals or desires are as important as my pursuit of an ever-deepening relationship with you.

May

Let the word of Christ dwell richly among you, in all wisdom teaching and admonishing one another through psalms, hymns, and spiritual songs, singing to God with gratitude in your hearts.

COLOSSIANS 3:16 CSB

Scripture Reading: 1 Chronicles 25-27

Called to Serve

The responsibility for the east gate went to Meshelemiah and his group. The north gate was assigned to his son Zechariah, a man of unusual wisdom.

1 Chronicles 26:14 NLT

There are sections throughout the Bible that celebrate people who use us their unique skillsets to work together to serve God. The reading plan for the devotional today is one of those sections. Aaron's descendants were serving as priests in organized groups according to their calling. Musicians were appointed to lead all of Israel in songs of worship. Men from several families were called up to be gatekeepers, watching over the people of Jerusalem and guarding against people who held malicious intent.

In any community there are a myriad of roles to fill. Everyone contributes in a different way, and each part is important. God asks each of us to fill our roles with humility and a willingness to follow his leadership in our lives. The more time we spend comparing our purpose to some else's, the less time we have to find the joy in what God has given us.

Lord, help me value the skills you've given me and the place you've called me to serve within your network of believers.

Scripture Reading: 1 Chronicles 28-29

From God

Wealth and honor come from you;
you are the ruler of all things.
In your hands are strength and power
to exalt and give strength to all.
1 Chronicles 29:12 niv

David's song of praise at the end of his life is a crescendo of everything he had come to know about God. His song roots God's salvation work in the story of Abraham, Isaac, and Jacob. He goes on to declare God's greatness, power, glory, majesty, and splendor. He had learned over his years that those qualities belonged to God alone.

God is our eternal source of goodness and provision. Every good gift we have comes from his hands. When we are strong, it's because God is upholding us with his might. He sustains, upholds, and equips his people. There is nothing we can do apart from him, and he is worthy of all our praise.

Lord, at the end of my life may these truths be deeply embedded in my soul.

Scripture Reading: 2 Chronicles 1-3

Revealing Question

That night God appeared to Solomon and said, "What do you want? Ask, and I will give it to you!"

2 Chronicles 1:7 NLT

"What do you want?" is a common question throughout the ministry of Jesus. He asked John the Baptist's disciples this question when they met him. He asked the blind man, Bartimaeus, the same question during their encounter. He asked a similar question to the blind man at the pool of Bethesda, and he also posed this question to the mother of two of his disciples.

How we answer that question reveals a lot about our hearts. Our desires show where our treasure lies. In Solomon's case, he answered that he wanted wisdom and knowledge to lead the people of Israel properly. It was a humble request that demonstrated his desire to serve God well and to honor the legacy that David had left him.

God, what is the true desire of my heart? What is it that I really want, and is it in line with what you want for my life?

Scripture Reading: 2 Chronicles 4-6

No One

"LORD, the God of Israel, there is no God like you in heaven or on earth—you who keep your covenant of love with your servants who continue wholeheartedly in your way."

2 CHRONICLES 6:14 NIV

Recurring throughout the Bible is the theological truth that there is no one like the God of Israel in all of heaven or on all the earth. God is unique in his identity and in his activity. There is no one else who has his perfection of character, and there is no one else whose actions are always just, loving, and wise. No one can compare to him.

God is all-powerful and all-knowing, yet he is willing to stoop down and make a covenant with humanity. He is holy, yet he is merciful toward us while we are sinners. He is loving and kind, yet he sent his son to embrace suffering he did not deserve. There truly is no one like our God.

Lord, you are so much greater, more loving, and more wondrous than I am able to comprehend. No one is like you God, overflowing with goodness and worthy of praise.

Scripture Reading: 2 Chronicles 7-9

Return to the Lord

"If my people who are called by my name will humble themselves and pray and seek my face and turn from their wicked ways, I will hear from heaven and will forgive their sins and restore their land."

2 Chronicles 7:14 NLT

The Lord knew his people would not always be faithful to walk with him. He knew they would get lost and make the wrong choices. He anticipated the wandering of his people, so he poured his heart out in encouragement. He addressed his people at the dedication of the temple. He reminded everyone that they could return to him no matter how far they wandered.

It takes humility for a man to admit he has gotten lost. It's embarrassing to recognize when we've made the wrong choice or wandered too far in the wrong direction. It might seem risky or uncomfortable, but admitting our faults is an essential step to being put back on the right path. God promises to lift us up no matter where we are when we turn to him.

Lord, may I have the courage to be humble. May I let down my guard and trust you for the direction of my life.

Scripture Reading: 2 Chronicles 10-12

Establishing a Kingdom

When the kingdom of Rehoboam was established and strong, he and all Israel with him abandoned the Law of the Lord.

2 Chronicles 12:1 NASB

Excessive power leading to corruption is a common story. This was most certainly true about Rehoboam. Once he seized control of the tribes of Israel he arrogantly proclaimed that he would rule more harshly and oppressively than his father. With a lust for dominance, he established his kingdom on the backs of the people.

His attempt to seize control ironically undermined his ability to do so. As he and the people gave up their relationship with God, God gave them up to outside conquerors. At one point the King of Egypt attacked Jerusalem and plundered the city, taking the gold treasuries from the temple. Rehoboam pretended to have complete authority for seventeen years, but he was an evil king who did not seek the Lord.

Lord, keep me from establishing my own kingdom in my own strength. Instead, I want to serve in your eternal kingdom for your glory.

Scripture Reading: 2 Chronicles 13-15

The Lord His God

Then Asa cried out to the LORD his God, "O LORD, no one but you can help the powerless against the mighty! Help us, O LORD our God, for we trust in you alone. It is in your name that we have come against this vast horde. O LORD, you are our God; do not let mere men prevail against you!"

2 CHRONICLES 14:11 NLT

Asa was a good king who did what was right in the eyes of the Lord. That did not mean that Asa didn't have to deal with his share of trouble, but it did mean that Asa did his best to serve the one true God. For Asa, following the Lord became a personal relationship. He asked God for help throughout his reign, and he trusted God above all else.

At one point the rampaging King of Ethiopia made his way to Jerusalem and attacked with one million men. As Asa deployed his soldiers, he must have known he was outmatched on the battlefield. So, he cried out to God for help. God heard him and defeated his enemies. After this miraculous victory, Asa led his people to trust the Lord personally and live courageously by the strength of his Spirit.

Strengthen my personal trust in you, my God.

Scripture Reading: 2 Chronicles 16-18

Stay Dependent

"The eyes of the LORD run to and fro throughout the whole earth, to give strong support to those whose heart is blameless toward him. You have done foolishly in this, for from now on you will have wars."

2 CHRONICLES 16:9 ESV

Instead of relying on God for one of his battles, Asa turned to an outside pagan kingdom for an allegiance of power. Afterward, God sent a prophet named Hanani to confront Asa. Instead of responding with repentance, Asa reacted in anger. He imprisoned Hanani and put him in stocks. Asa also began oppressing his people and eventually died miserably rejecting the Lord's help.

What causes a good man to fall? What leads a faithful man to go astray? Somewhere along the line Asa decided that God's help wasn't enough. He looked for strength somewhere else. Maybe he felt like he could control the situation if he handled it himself. Maybe he wanted to see evidence of an allegiance with his own eyes. Either way, he took things into his own hands when he should have stayed dependent on God. He turned away from God and pridefully ignored the opportunities he had to repent.

Lord, may I stay true to you for the rest of my life. Don't let me fall.

Scripture Reading: 2 Chronicles 19-21

Trustworthy Law

"Let the fear of the LORD be on you. Judge carefully, for with the LORD our God there is no injustice or partiality or bribery."

2 CHRONICLES 19:7 NIV

King Jehosophat imparted some wise advice to his regional judges. He reminded them to render verdicts that reflected the justice of the Lord. He told them that their decrees represented the character and heart of God, so they should fear the Lord and judge with integrity.

Jehosophat knew that the Law of God was very clear about keeping the court systems pure and trustworthy. To pervert the system of justice was to subvert the kingdom of Israel. God cares about justice, innocence, and fair systems. It is wise to pray for the judges of our nation. We can pray for justice in our court systems and integrity among our lawmakers. The presence of corruption should not hinder our prayers but urge us to stand up for what is right.

Lord, help our judges and our courts of law be pleasing in your sight. May those who make and uphold our laws be people of integrity and who give reverence to you.

Scripture Reading: 2 Chronicles 22-24

Personal Faith

Joash did what was right in the sight of the LORD all the days of Jehoiada the priest.

2 CHRONICLES 24:2 NASB

As long as Jehoiada was alive, Joash did what was right in the sight of the Lord. The priest provided a stable reminder to Joash that God was real. Joash, collaborating with Jehoiada, even started to repair and restore the temple. When Jehoiada died at a very old age, Joash and the leaders of Israel held so much respect for all the good he had done that they buried him among the kings of Israel in the City of David.

Unfortunately, Joash abandoned his faith once Jehoiada was gone. Joash had leaned on the faith of his priest but failed to develop his own personal relationship with God. Almost immediately Joash and his leaders made a deliberate choice to stop worshipping the Lord to start following other gods. The life of Joash is a reminder of how important it is to develop a personal relationship with God rather than depending on the faith of someone else.

God, I need to grow in my walk with you. Strengthen my relationship with you and increase my faith.

Scripture Reading: 2 Chronicles 25-27

Two Ways

King Jotham became powerful because he was careful to live in obedience to the LORD his God.

2 CHRONICLES 27:6 NLT

There are two ways to become powerful in this world. The first is to seize power. This is the way of Satan, who tried to steal glory for himself in heaven and then tried to gain influence over humanity through deception. This way is alluring because it gives a person an intimidating and impressive outward image of power.

The second way to become powerful is through a posture of obedience. This is the way of Jesus. He teaches us that God's strength is far above our own, and we are called to humbly submit to his ways. We have access to the unshakeable kingdom through the sacrifice of Christ. Our power doesn't come from our own abilities. We are strong and powerful because of the long-suffering of Jesus.

Lord, give me the courage of King Jotham, who walked obediently with you. May my pursuit of power be defined by the laying down of my life.

Scripture Reading: 2 Chronicles 28-30

Reforming a Kingdom

In the first year of his reign, in the first month, he opened the doors of the LORD's temple and repaired them.

2 CHRONICLES 29:3 CSB

Hezekiah declared the purpose of his reign immediately. His reign, through both proclamation and action, would prioritize a resilient commitment to God. The first thing he did was open the temple to the people of Jerusalem and initiate a campaign of restoration. The prior king, his father Ahaz, had led the people of Judah into sin. During that time, the temple had fallen into disuse and disrepair. The neglected condition of the temple reflected the neglected condition of Judah's faith in God.

Hezekiah was determined that his kingdom would be different. He valued the covenant his people had with God, and he sought to restore it. It took courage for him to rid the land of his father's habits and submit once again to the Lord. He boldly shifted the course of his kingdom despite the patterns that were already in place.

Lord, let a reformation that begins within me spread to those around me. Give me courage to change ungodly patterns in my life no matter how well rooted they are.

Scripture Reading: 2 Chronicles 31-33

He Prospered

In everything that he undertook in the service of God's temple and in obedience to the law and the commands, he sought his God and worked wholeheartedly. And so he prospered.

2 Chronicles 31:21 NIV

A man who honors God is a man who has a personal commitment to the Lord. Throughout history we see that men who sought God and worked wholeheartedly in their calling were men who prospered in their leadership, family, and career. Furthermore, anyone who chose to walk beside those men flourished.

The reverse is also true. Namely, men who sought after their own gain left a trail of chaos and distress behind them. This repeated pattern continues to capture men in its trap despite its destructive tendencies. It takes bold men like Hezekiah to break the cycle of greediness that leads to ruin. We each must decide what kind of man we will be.

God, give me boldness to seek after you. When temptation begins to lure me away, pull me back into an obedient walk with you.

Scripture Reading: 2 Chronicles 34-36

Pattern of Neglect

When the king heard what was written in the Law, he tore his clothes in despair.

2 CHRONICLES 34:19 NLT

After Hezekiah died, his son Manasseh became king and did evil in the Lord's sight. Manasseh's long reign had a terrible impact on the people of Judah. He popularized pagan shrines and led the population away from God. As result, God allowed the Assyrian army to ransack Jerusalem and take Manasseh hostage to Babylon. The Assyrians put a ring through his nose and bound him in chains.

When Manasseh's son, Amon, became king, he continued in the evil practices of his father, and it became a bloodbath. He was so terrible that his own officials assassinated him. The citizens of Judah then executed the officials. By the time Amon's son became king, the people had forgotten all about God's Word.

Lord, do not let me fall away from you and your commands. Keep me close. I pray that I will never forget your Word.

Scripture Reading: Ezra 1-3

Longing for Home

Then rose up the heads of the fathers' houses of Judah and Benjamin, and the priests and the Levites, everyone whose spirit God had stirred to go up to rebuild the house of the LORD that is in Jerusalem.

EZRA 1:5 ESV

God's people wandered away from him while they were in exile. They turned to worship other gods and neglected their commitment the Lord, so he sent other nations to conquer them and scatter them throughout what we now call the Middle East. After a couple generations passed, the people began to long for God again. They grew in their desire to follow his commands and restore his temple. Their hearts were stirred to return home.

Most of us can only imagine what it would be like to wander in a land we don't know. We can assume what it might be like to long for a place where our hearts feel at home. The reality is that we are all strangers in a foreign land. Our true home is with the Lord, and we won't be satisfied until we are with him face to face.

God, reign over my life. Stir my heart for you and fill me with joy and satisfaction in your presence.

Scripture Reading: Ezra 4-6

God's Kingdom

"We are the servants of the God of heaven and earth, and we are rebuilding the temple that was built many years ago, one that a great king of Israel built and finished."

EZRA 5:11 NIV

It had been hundreds of years since Solomon built the temple. Since then, the people of Israel and Judah had waffled in their faith. They often chose to completely reject the God of their ancestors. Now, there was rabble of faithful followers of the Lord who sensed a calling to return home to Jerusalem to rebuild the temple.

There was plenty of opposition to their endeavor. Enemies did not want the Jews reestablished in Jerusalem. Occupying forces did not want the walls to be rebuilt, yet the resilient faith of determined men led to God's reign being established in the Promised Land. These men shrewdly used every tool at their disposal whether it was political, financial, or material. Their tenacity resulted in the first Passover celebration in several generations.

Lord, forgive me for my short-sighted faith. Empower me with boldness to persistently seek your kingdom on earth as it is in heaven.

Scripture Reading: Ezra 7-10

Starting Over

"Ezra, according to God's wisdom that you possess, appoint magistrates and judges to judge all the people in the region west of the Euphrates who know the laws of your God and to teach anyone who does not know them."

EZRA 7:25 CSB

Ezra was recognized as a priest and a teacher of God's law. He had been given authority both by the people of Judah and by King Artaxerxes to restore an operating government in Jerusalem. Under his leadership, many gifted leaders returned from Babylon to Jerusalem to establish this new government. Ezra was able to convene people to start over in the Promised Land.

After so many years of wandering and pain, the people of God were once again taking root in the land the Lord had given to Abraham. Ezra and the leaders with him were determined that the people would confess their sin and declare their desire to follow the commands of the Lord. He was dedicated to helping the people honor God.

Heavenly Father, help me take advantage of every opportunity I have to follow you. Thank you for the people in my life who encourage me to honor you.

Scripture Reading: Nehemiah 1-3

End of the Exile

When I heard this, I sat down and wept. In fact, for days I mourned, fasted, and prayed to the God of heaven.

Nehemiah 1:4 NLT

As part of the rebuilding campaign in Jerusalem, King Artaxerxes of Babylon gave his trusted cupbearer, Nehemiah, permission to return to the Promised Land. Nehemiah was his poison taster, so the king relied daily on Nehemiah for his very life. The king also benefited from having many capable Jewish leaders impacting communities throughout his kingdom. To lose these individuals to an endeavor as daunting as rebuilding a city his predecessors had destroyed was not something to be dismissive about.

When Artaxerxes saw Nehemiah's broken heart and heard his impassioned plea, he chose to consent to Nehemiah's plan to rebuild Jerusalem. The king initiated the end of the exile, and he funded the beginning of the restoration of Jerusalem. Nehemiah set off on his expedition and organized hundreds of gifted and passionately committed men to join him in his efforts.

God, I'm inspired by the resilient faith of the men in Ezra and Nehemiah. Help me build strong character and unwavering faith.

Scripture Reading: Nehemiah 4-6

The Right Posture

Remember, O my God, all that I have done for these people, and bless me for it.

NEHEMIAH 5:19 NLT

Nehemiah faced one obstacle after another in his efforts to rebuild Jerusalem. Though he had the backing of King Artaxerxes, he did not have an easy time with local and regional officials. The enemies of the kingdom of Judah did not want to see Jerusalem restored to its former glory, but Nehemiah wouldn't be deterred.

When some intimidating men wanted to oppress the families and workers who were trying to settle in the land, Nehemiah defied them. He encouraged everyone around him to stay focused on the Lord. He also didn't put a tax burden on the citizens of the land, choosing instead to find his own funding for his government. His courage and integrity inspired others who agreed to follow through with their promises to restore Jerusalem.

Lord, help me stay focused on the job you've given me. Give me courage to follow you with integrity and honor. Help me lead others toward greater obedience to you.

Scripture Reading: Nehemiah 7-9

The Gathered Assembly

They read out of the book of the law of God, translating and giving the meaning so that the people could understand what was read.

NEHEMIAH 8:8 CSB

Ezra was the high priest in the newly restored temple of Jerusalem. The entire community gathered after being scattered for several generations, and they listened to him read the words of Moses. Ezra stood on a platform where everyone could see him and hear him, and when he opened the scroll, the assembly rose to their feet. There was great respect for the word of God.

As Ezra began to read, teachers began to explain the meaning of the words in the book of the law. Then, Nehemiah encouraged people not to weep over the years where the word of God had been lost, but to rejoice. He knew that the posture of their hearts as they returned to the Lord mattered more than a past they couldn't change.

Lord, help me focus on your Word today. Fill me with praise and teach me how to honor your name.

Scripture Reading: Nehemiah 10-11

Willing to Serve

The people commended all who volunteered to live in Jerusalem.

NEHEMIAH 11:2 NIV

The Lord invites us to serve alongside him. He includes us in his plans, and he gives us opportunities to partner with his purposes. He does not force us into labor but encourages us to use the skills and passions he's given us in service to others. He has called each of us to join him in his work of shepherding and restoration.

In the eleventh chapter of Nehemiah, there is tremendous respect for those who voluntarily give up their time and commitments to respond to the Lord's call to serve. In this case, people chose to leave their homes to resettle in Jerusalem and help with the restoration process. Several thousand people responded to the invitation and served in positions such as priests, administrators, gatekeepers, and musicians.

Lord, show me opportunities to serve you. Help me use the skills you've given me to help others.

Scripture Reading: Nehemiah 12-13

Once Again

Long ago in the days of David and Asaph there were directors of the singers, and there were songs of praise and thanksgiving to God.

NEHEMIAH 12:46 ESV

One of the best things about rebuilding the temple and reinstating the religious system in Jerusalem was that the practice of worshipping through the psalms was restored. A team of musicians and choir directors was commissioned to lead the gathering of God's people once again. It was during this time that the book of Psalms as we know it today took shape. The psalms of David, Asaph, Moses, and the Sons of Korah were sung once again in the Promised Land.

Engaging in worship through songs of praise has been the practice of God's people for thousands of years. However, we have the privilege of having unlimited access to God's Word. We don't have to wait for someone to lead us in worship or remind us of what God has said. We can open our Bible at any time and lift an offering of praise to the Lord.

Lord, fill my heart with praise today. Thank you for the gift of your Word.

Scripture Reading: Esther 1-3

Orchestrating Events

At that time there was a Jewish man in the fortress of Susa whose name was Mordecai son of Jair. He was from the tribe of Benjamin and was a descendant of Kish and Shimei.

Esther 2:5 NLT

Esther is the only book in Bible that does not mention God. His name is never used, yet for thousands of years people have recognized that God's hands were at work in Esther's story. He orchestrated the rescue of his people through Esther's courageous actions. It's a testimony to the fact that God is always moving even when it seems less obvious.

God's work in our lives won't always follow our expectations. He is not bound by our perceptions or beholden to our way of doing things. He doesn't have to work within our timing or at the locations we specify. He does as he pleases, and his ability to weave his story together is greater than we can understand.

God, thank you for accomplishing your will in this world even when I can't comprehend all that you are doing. I trust you.

Scripture Reading: Esther 4-6

God's Brilliance

"Go at once," the king commanded Haman. "Get the robe and the horse and do just as you have suggested for Mordecai the Jew, who sits at the king's gate. Do not neglect anything you have recommended."

Esther 6:10 NIV

When we think about God's character traits, we might not include wit in our list. Even though it is not mentioned explicitly, we can see it on full display in the book of Esther. The unexpected twist in the story that leads to Haman's embarrassment is a great example. This moment of surprising triumph for Esther and Mordecai coupled with the Haman's humiliation is one of many moments of punchy brilliance throughout the Bible.

God is not boring or dry. His Word is not empty or meaningless. His character is full and perfect. He is the epitome of everything good. He is wise, joyful, strong, smart, funny, and kind. We get a more accurate picture of who he is when we remember that his perfection is not limited to being powerful or mighty. He is bigger and better than we often give him credit for.

Lord, help me see your creative and surprising work in my life today. Don't let me grow stale in my practice of faith!

Scripture Reading: Esther 7-8

God's Plans

For the Jews there was light, joy, jubilation, and honor.
ESTHER 8:16 NASB

The Jewish people had lost their homeland and were taken hostage and scattered. They were a breath away from total genocide, so saying they had a good reason to celebrate is an immense understatement. Their enemy had been found guilty of insurrection against God's people and had been executed. They were rescued from evil and liberated by the courageous actions of Esther.

God's plans for salvation will never be thwarted. His plans are trustworthy and true. What seems impossible to us is possible for God. His promises are true, and his faithfulness continues from generation to generation. He has given all of us endless reasons to celebrate.

God, I will not take your promises of restoration for granted. I know you will do what you say you will do.

Scripture Reading: Esther 9-10

Mordecai's Legacy

Mordecai the Jew was second only to King Ahasuerus. He was famous among the Jews and highly esteemed by many of his relatives. He continued to pursue prosperity for his people and to speak for the well-being of all his descendants.

Esther 10:3 CSB

To this day, Mordecai's courage and determination has helped Jewish people remember who they are and what they have experienced. Though they have often been overlooked due to their size and position, they have also been a people who have overcome tremendous odds. Over thousands of years, the Jewish people have survived repeated genocide attempts. They have often been displaced from their land and scattered around the globe.

While God's plan and purpose for his people are evident throughout the book of Esther, his name is omitted. There can be a tendency to find one's identity in accomplishments of the past but fail to recognize the One who orchestrated the victories. Let's be faithful to remember that God's hand has been and always will be at work.

Lord, help me remember that you hold everything together in your power. I trust your plans.

Scripture Reading: Job 1-4

Unanswered Questions

Then the LORD asked Satan, "Have you noticed my servant Job? He is the finest man in all the earth. He is blameless—a man of complete integrity. He fears God and stays away from evil."

JOB 1:8 NLT

As we read Job we might wonder why God draws attention to him. It seems like he paints a target on his back. Why would he put Job in the spotlight for Satan to attack him? One of the most difficult underlying struggles of the book of Job is why God allows suffering and pain to harm his people.

The book of Job is not for the faint of heart. It's okay to read it and have more questions than we began with. God is not frustrated by our questions or doubts. We aren't the first people to misunderstand the work of the Lord, and we won't be the last. We might not get all the answers we want, but we can strive to trust in the Lord's goodness despite the things we don't understand.

Lord, I am realizing it is more important for me to seek after you than it is to seek after answers. May my heart be secure and satisfied in your presence.

Scripture Reading: Job 5-8

Raw Emotion

"I loathe my life; I would not live forever.
Leave me alone, for my days are a breath."
JOB 7:16 ESV

The Bible does not shy away from raw human emotions. Some passages reveal unbridled joy that spills over the pages while others jump deeply into the minefield of doubt and depression. Many verses in the book of Job give voice to the deepest, darkest feelings of grief and loss. Job is a book that details the agony of mourning and the pain of wrestling with suffering that can't be understood.

There's no need to shy away from the raw expressions of emotion found in the Bible. These passages are evidence that God understands the human experience. They remind us that God is not afraid to encounter our extreme emotions. As the book of Job reveals, God loves us when we think we are holding everything together and when we are falling apart.

Lord, thank you for being consistent and faithful even when I feel like a mess. Thank you for holding all of my emotions with kindness and strength.

Scripture Reading: Job 9-12

Holy God

"If only there were someone to mediate between us,
someone to bring us together,
someone to remove God's rod from me,
so that his terror would frighten me no more."

Job 9:33-34 NIV

Job's cry echoes the cries of all those who discover that they cannot save themselves. No one can rescue themselves from the holy judgment of God. No one is innocent before a holy God. His perception is perfect, and he executes his will flawlessly. We might be full of questions, but we must acknowledge that our understanding is finite while God's is infinite.

We will end up exhausted and isolated if our faith is based on our questions being answered the way we want. There must come a point where we surrender to the one true God. We will all face a critical point in our lives when we must choose between our own understanding and trust in the Lord. Our reverence for who he is must take a higher seat than our questioning.

Jesus, you are holy, and I am not. Help me trust you even when I don't understand.

Scripture Reading: Job 13-15

Resurrection Hope

"When a person dies, will he come back to life?
If so, I would wait all the days of my struggle
until my relief comes."

JOB 14:14 CSB

Considering all that Job has experienced, it was appropriate for him to consider what happens after death. His observations on the frailty of humanity make perfect sense. He was so exhausted from his pain and misery that he flirted with the idea that death would be preferable to his current state. As such, he wanted to know if there is a resurrection after a person dies.

The agonized pondering of his soul is met with disdain from his friend, Eliphaz. He is short-tempered and impatient with Job's misery. Eliphaz didn't understand that Job's question sits at the heart of God's salvation plan. God's eternal and glorious plan is that the dead will be raised! He assures us all that suffering will end, and evil will be overcome. The core of the gospel message is found vibrantly within the book of Job.

Lord, thank you for promising life after death. Fill me with the hope of resurrection and help me stay faithful to you.

Scripture Reading: Job 16-18

Faithful Friends

"My eyes are red with weeping;
dark shadows circle my eyes.
Yet I have done no wrong,
and my prayer is pure."
Job 16:16-17 NLT

Job's life hadn't always been so miserable. There was a time when he had everything he could have ever wanted. His family was intact and healthy. His career was successful, and his reputation was solid. Though he didn't know it while he was suffering, he would have all of that again. In the midst of his agony, restoration seemed impossible and far off. Knowing things would get better didn't help his immediate suffering.

When people suffer, it is tempting to remind them of what's good. It's tempting to pat them on the back and tell them it will get better. The truth is that people often need presence over perspective. In other words, showing up for people who are hurting is more important than making sure they see things rightly. We don't have to convince those who are grieving that their grief won't last forever. Instead, we can sit with them in it and offer comfort and companionship.

Lord, help me be a good friend to those who are suffering.

"Blessed are those who hear the word of God and keep it."

Luke 11:28 CSB

Scripture Reading: Job 19-21

My Redeemer Lives

"I know that my Redeemer lives,
and at the end he will stand on the dust.
Even after my skin has been destroyed,
yet I will see God in my flesh."

Job 19:25-26 CSB

Job believed that God was living and active. Even though his life was surrounded by decay and destruction, Job knew that God would bring life from death. He was confident that God was alive and able to intervene on his behalf. He knew that God would not be satisfied to leave him in his despair forever.

Job looked forward to the day when his life would be fully restored. He knew that God, by his very nature, desired that none should perish. God created this world and would never allow it to spin out of control. God will bring all things back under his perfect and protective care. If you find yourself struggling today, remember that your Redeemer lives, and he has not forsaken you.

Jesus, my Redeemer, thank you for caring for me and giving me everlasting life.

Scripture Reading: Job 22-24

Petitioning God

"If only I knew where to find him;
if only I could go to his dwelling!"
JOB 23:3 NIV

Job felt wronged by his situation. He had done nothing immoral, yet he had lost everything. He also felt wronged by his friends. He had been forced to listen to their accusations and arrogance even while he wallowed in the misery of his despair. When Job suffered, he called upon the Lord. He cried out in despair, and he mused about where God might be in the midst of his pain.

Knowing where to find the Judge of the world and how to talk with him is key to being able to bring a petition before him. After all, the conversation Job has with his friends is not ultimately the conversation he needed to have. The conversation he needed to have was with God. When we are suffering, we must recognize that God alone is our help and strength.

Lord, thank you for listening to my frustrations and complaints. Thank you for listening and being there for me.

Scripture Reading: Job 25-27

Speak Accurately

"As long as my breath is in me,
and the spirit of God is in my nostrils,
my lips will not speak falsehood,
and my tongue will not utter deceit."
Job 27:3-4 ESV

Job was under duress, and his suffering was unprecedented, yet he refused to manipulate his words or exaggerate his condition. He did not want to be found guilty of wrongdoing. He did not want to speak inappropriately against his friends, and he did not want to tell a false story to win people over to his side. Job knew that a man in trouble will bring further misery upon himself if others distrust his what he says. Instead, he chose to trust God rather than twist his speech to gain sympathy.

It is possible to maintain integrity and character in the midst of pain. It can be tempting to allow ourselves extra margin because we are hurting, giving allowances for tendencies we might not be okay with otherwise. It's important to speak honestly, maintain honor, and pursue holiness in all circumstances.

Lord, may maturity mark my mouth. When I speak, let my words be trustworthy and true.

Scripture Reading: Job 28-30

Go Directly to God

"I cry to you, O God, but you don't answer.
I stand before you, but you don't even look."
JOB 30:20 NLT

Job's friends kept trying to engage him in arguments. They expected him to be fully swayed by their brilliant inquiries and keen insights. By the thirtieth chapter of the book, they had only succeeded in exasperating him. Over the course of their visits, Job had grown tired of their relentless debates.

Job felt that his friends misinterpreted his situation. Furthermore, they didn't have the power to do anything about his misery anyway. It just wasn't worth trying to defend himself to them. What Job really wanted to do was to deal with God directly, for God was the one who could explain why all this had happened to him and offer relief. He believed that God could handle his cries and provide true answers to his dilemma.

Lord, help me turn to you above all else. Remind me that turning to you is better than having unproductive conversations with friends.

Scripture Reading: Job 31-33

Trusting God

"If I have walked with deception,
And my foot has hurried after deceit,
Let Him weigh me with accurate scales,
And let God know my integrity."

Job 31:5-6 NASB

Job's friends determined that he must have sinned in order for all this trouble to fall upon him. They continuously challenged his claims of innocence. Their theology didn't allow them to understand that Job had been suffering because the world was caught up in an ongoing spiritual battle. They couldn't comprehend that the devil was intent on causing pain and disrupting people's connection to God. As a result, Job's friends judged him.

Job continued to trust God despite his friend's doubts. He relied on God's judgment over his friend's. Job displays resilient faith in the midst of tragic and painful circumstances. He trusted that God had a bigger, eternal plan even when he didn't understand how it would play out. He knew that God was ultimately trustworthy.

God, I lay myself before you today. Search me and know my ways. Point out anything in me that is offensive to you. Help me walk humbly in the grace of my Savior.

Scripture Reading: Job 34-36

All-knowing God

"God is exalted in his power.
Who is a teacher like him?"
JOB 36:22 NIV

Job's friend Elihu hadn't been right about everything he said to Job, but he was certainly right about one thing. God is greater than any other being. There is no one in heaven or on earth who compares to the Lord. He is high above everyone else in knowledge, power, and love. While Job cried to the Lord and was full of questions, Elihu urged him to keep a proper perspective about God's position of glory.

What Elihu struggled to appreciate, however, is that Job desired to have God as his teacher precisely for that reason. Only God could help Job understand why such terrible things had happened. Job recognized his omniscient power and trusted him to see him through.

Lord, I seek you because I need you. I don't understand why things happen the way they do, but I put my faith in you. Lead me and guide me so that I might honor you all of my days.

Scripture Reading: Job 37-39

Our Great God

"Where were you when I laid the foundation of the earth? Tell me, if you have understanding."

Job 38:4 ESV

The chapters for today's reading are some of the most compelling theological truths in all of the Bible. It is hard not to be humbled before the Lord as he asks question after question, revealing his eternal glory and calling attention to our impermanence. God describes his majesty, creativity, and awesome capability. We stand at the mercy of our Creator who formed the dimensions of the heavens and made boundaries for the oceans.

God is great, yet he stoops to talk with us. He is mindful of his creation, yet he calls us to be mindful of our position. He is thoughtful and kind, and he is worthy of our humble worship. Our souls are most satisfied when we are aware of his greatness in conjunction with his mercy.

Lord, I am humbled in your presence today. Thank you for engaging me in conversation even though I don't come close to deserving you. You are an amazing God!

Scripture Reading: Job 40-42

Covering My Mouth

"I am nothing—how could I ever find the answers?
I will cover my mouth with my hand.
I have said too much already.
I have nothing more to say."

Job 40:3-5 NLT

Job held his own during the torrent of challenging arguments from his friends. He was able to respond with clarity, conviction, truth, and passion. His friends could not persuade him to concede, but Job was left speechless before the Lord. He didn't have an answer for God. His questions were too profound, awe-inspiring, and humbling for Job to continue arguing.

At a certain point we run out of things to say to God. We can express our messy thoughts and feelings, but eventually we stand laid bare before him. We can hurl our questions and disappointments at him, but eventually we will be humbled and quiet. God graciously listens to everything we have to say, and he faithfully draws us toward him in kindness. He doesn't shame us for our big emotions, and he wisely reminds us his greatness compared to our humanity.

Lord, in my grumbling and despair, remind me of your greatness. Help me be quiet and listen to what you must tell me.

Scripture Reading: Psalms 1-4

Stand Tall

They delight in the law of the LORD,
meditating on it day and night.
They are like trees planted along the riverbank,
bearing fruit each season.

PSALM 1:2-3 NLT

Each day we can choose to stand in the company of the wicked or we can seek righteousness. We can follow the alluring promises of the world, or we can trust in God's promises. Those who pursue the ways of the wicked end up being blown about by the winds of deceit and worry because they have not rooted themselves in the fertile ground of God's righteousness. Their souls become dry, barren, and lacking the nourishment of God.

In contrast, those who choose to follow the ways of God become like strong trees planted by fresh, running water. They remain steady because they have rooted themselves in healthy soil. They stand firm through every season, and their lives overflow with fruitfulness. They remain youthful in spirit and are successful in all they commit themselves to do.

Lord, may I delight in the nourishment of your Word as I read through the book of Psalms. Help me stand tall as I trust in your commands.

Scripture Reading: Psalms 5-8

At the Start

In the morning, LORD, You will hear my voice;
In the morning I will present my prayer to You and be on the watch.

PSALM 5:3 NASB

David started each day in prayer. He would begin the morning by bringing his requests to God. In this psalm, David reveals that he would speak to God and ask God to lead him down the right path. He committed himself to the Lord, and he took the time to acknowledge God's unfailing love. He brought his needs before the Lord, and he asked for protection against his enemies.

It is good to establish a morning routine. Beginning our day in the presence of the Lord sets our trajectory for the rest of the day. It allows us to begin with a lighter heart and a clearer mind. Each new day is an opportunity to give him our burdens and trust that he can handle them. We set ourselves up for success when we offer him our praise and keep our eyes on him despite what happens.

Lord, I want to spend time with you every single day of my life. Help me build a routine of prayer in my daily schedule.

Scripture Reading: Psalms 9-12

Get to Know Him

Those who know your name trust in you,
for you, LORD, have never forsaken those who seek you.
PSALM 9:10 NIV

David's heart erupts with adoration for God in Psalm 9. His soul is satisfied as he declares his praise and sings a song of worship. He recognizes that God reigns forever, and he can see that God provides refuge for those in need. David has learned that God judges the world in fairness and offers mercy to those who search for him. As such, he overflows with worship for all the amazing things God has done.

Here in verse ten, David rejoices in his faith because he is blessed to know God by name. He is so thankful that he knows God personally! He recognizes how great God is because he has spent time getting to know him. He is grateful for the relationship he's built, and he is humbled by God's willingness to call him a friend.

God, thank you for letting me get to know you personally. The more I know you, the more I am overwhelmed by how great you are!

Scripture Reading: Psalms 13-16

Because of Jesus

O Lord, who shall sojourn in you tent?
Who shall dwell on your holy hill?

Psalm 15:1 ESV

Only those who are without sin are worthy to approach the Lord to worship him. God is holy and there is no sin in him. He is perfect, pure, and without blemish. How could anyone who has used their hands, lips, or minds to sin then use things to praise God? Psalm 15 emphasizes that only those who are blameless can enter the presence of the Lord. This truth forces the necessary question of whether or not anyone is worthy to be near him.

We are filled with praise because Jesus is the answer to our greatest problem! His death and resurrection allows us to take his righteousness as our own. He made a way for us to be completely at home in the presence of the perfect Father. We can be near God without hindrance because of what Christ has done.

Jesus, thank you for dying on the cross to take away my sin and make me blameless. I am not worthy of you, but you have made me worthy. I will praise you forever!

Scripture Reading: Psalms 17-20

All of Creation

May the words of my mouth
and the meditation of my heart
be pleasing to you,
O LORD, my rock and my redeemer.
PSALM 19:14 NLT

Psalm 19 is known as one of the many "Creation Psalms" that are spread throughout the entire book. These psalms highlight how God's creation points to his wonder and glory, leading humanity to humility and praise. The very existence of the world around us is more than enough to draw us to ongoing worship and wonder.

The stars in the sky and the wonders of the heavens work together in unison to proclaim praise to God. Creation speaks without using words, testifying loudly to the greatness of God. Humans around the planet are drawn to marvel at God because of the message creation broadcast. As David ponders all of this, he realizes that his own mouth must also speak in a way that honors the Lord. He is stirred by the wonder of the world, and he is convicted to announce the Lord's greatness alongside the rest of creation.

O Lord, my rock and my redeemer, may the words of my mouth and meditation of my heart be pleasing to you!

Scripture Reading: Psalms 21-24

Our Shepherd

Even though I walk through the darkest valley,
I will fear no evil, for you are with me;
your rod and your staff, they comfort me.
Psalm 23:4 NIV

In this famous Psalm, David declares that the Lord is his shepherd. The Lord is the one who leads him to restoration and peace, renews his strength, guides him through life, and gives him honor. David declares that the Shepherd is with him even in times of danger and despair. He protects him and brings him comfort no matter what is going on around him. He even goes so far as to prepare him a great feast in the presence of his enemies.

As the Good Shepherd, Jesus promised to protect and comfort his sheep. In fact, he said he would lay down his life for his sheep. He promised that his sheep would know his voice and that he would give them peace in all circumstances.

Jesus, you are my Shepherd. Thank you for protecting me today and leading me through ever season I face.

Scripture Reading: Psalms 25-28

Dwell With God

One thing I have asked from the Lord, that I shall seek:
That I may dwell in the house of the Lord
all the days of my life,
To behold the beauty of the Lord
And to meditate in His temple.

Psalm 27:4 NASB

Imagine if we could each live exactly where we wanted. Some of us would likely choose a sandy beach or a mountainside cabin. We choose something that stirred up joy in our hearts and contentment in our spirits. We'd choose something that we found to be inspiring or beautiful. We would pick out our individual ideal situation.

The one place that came to mind for David was the house of the Lord. God's presence was his highest desire. He longed to be with God above anything or anyone else. He knew that only God's presence could provide him with the satisfaction he longed for. He knew that he was made to be close to his Creator. Without his Maker, nothing else seemed appealing.

Lord, may I never forget that my truest home is in your presence. May my heart long to be with you forever.

Scripture Reading: Psalms 29-32

Confessing Guilt

Finally, I confessed all my sins to you
and stopped trying to hide my guilt.
I said to myself, "I will confess my rebellion to the Lord."
And you forgave me! All my guilt is gone.

Psalm 32:5 NLT

There is no point in trying to hide our sin from God. He sees it all. In fact, he sees more of our sin than we can even recognize. He sees the sins we commit outright and the ones we commit mindlessly. He sees the deliberate lies we tell and the ones that sneak through our subconscious. He has a full and complete picture of our sins and intentions.

God's awareness of our guilt is not an excuse to avoid confession. It's also not meant to stir up shame or embarrassment. God's awareness of our sin should make us feel seen, known, and loved. He understands all of our flaws, yet he loves us fully. His perspective is untarnished, yet he still chooses to have mercy on us. We can openly confess our sins because we already know how he will respond.

Lord, I am sorry for my sin. Thank you for taking my sin away through the Cross. Please forgive me and make me new.

Scripture Reading: Psalms 33-36

By His Word

By the word of the LORD the heavens were made,
and by the breath of his mouth all their host.
PSALM 33:6 ESV

It took over seven years and over one hundred and fifty thousand laborers to build Solomon's temple. It took four years and twenty-one thousand workers to complete the Hoover Dam. It took ten years and one-and-a-half million people to complete the Suez Canal. It took ten years and four hundred thousand engineers, contractors, and support staff to land a manned capsule on the moon.

God took six days to create the entire universe with his voice. He simply spoke, and it came into being. Each of his declarations resulted in another glorious aspect of creation. Light, space, water, land, vegetation, and fauna were perfectly formed how he intended. He miraculously breathed life into all he created, and our response should be unending worship.

Lord, you alone deserve my praise. Your works are wonderous, and I am in awe of you.

Scripture Reading: Psalms 37-40

Be Still

Be still before the Lord
and wait patiently for him;
do not fret when people succeed in their ways,
when they carry out their wicked schemes.

Psalm 37:7 NIV

Many of us are overwhelmed with worry about what is happening in the world. We are overcome by unhealthy anxiety about the hostilities in our society, and we are frustrated that the wicked seem to prosper and flourish. It seems like it's only getting worse, and we struggle to maintain our view of the big picture.

When we are tempted to worry, Psalm 37 gives us hope. We can recognize that God is holding the future firmly in his hands. He knows exactly what is happening, and he encourages us to trust him. His plans have not been foiled, and his promises will stand true. He knows that we are discouraged when the wicked prosper, and he reassures us to keep our eyes on him. He will make everything right in his perfect timing.

Lord, I pray that my faith in you will be stronger than my worry today. Help me trust you even when I am discouraged.

Scripture Reading: Psalms 41-44

Hope in God

Why, my soul, are you so dejected?
Why are you in such turmoil?
Put your hope in God, for I will still praise him,
my Savior and my God.
PSALM 42:11 CSB

The writer of this psalm has a downcast spirit. While he can identify some reasons for why he might be sad, he can't find enough reason to continue to be. His circumstances are far from perfect, yet he still acknowledges that there isn't anything bad enough to keep him from praising God. He commands his soul to praise the Lord despite how he feels.

Today's psalm is a powerful reminder that we don't have to be controlled by our feelings. We can acknowledge them, give them to the Lord, and rise above them. We can praise him despite our suffering. We can command our very souls to rise up and worship our Maker. There is something incredibly powerful about turning our eyes toward the Lord when our flesh is crying out. As we direct our soul to the Lord, he faithfully blesses us with his presence.

God, I choose to put my hope in you today. Help me choose to worship you no matter what is happening around me.

Scripture Reading: Psalms 45-48

Be Still And Know

"Be still, and know that I am God!
I will be honored by every nation.
I will be honored throughout the world."
PSALM 46:10 NLT

Our modern society is addicted to being busy. We fill every free moment with entertainment rather than embracing the quiet. We amuse ourselves with mindless activity, and we occupy our minds with hectic thoughts. We have forgotten how to rest.

Stillness is a foreign concept for many people. No wonder we often feel distant from God. He is not frantic, chaotic, or hustling to accomplish the next item on his to do list. His presence is steady, quiet, and strong. If we quiet ourselves and make space to listen for his voice, we will hear it. If we give him our time, he will not disappoint us.

Lord, forgive me for making the busyness of my life seem more important than my relationship with you. Help me pause my activity and be still in your presence today.

Scripture Reading: Psalms 49-52

Cleanse Me

Be gracious to me, God,
according to your faithful love;
according to your abundant compassion,
blot out my rebellion.

PSALM 51:1 CSB

David was caught in his sin. He was confronted by his trusted advisor, and he admitted his wrongdoing. He was the king of Israel, so he could have tried to deny it. He could have used his power and influence to cover up his mistakes. He could have tried to defend himself or defame his advisor.

There are many paths David could have chosen when confronted with his sin, but David knew that God knew. David recognized that God was aware of every evil thing he had done, so he broke down and pleaded for mercy. He begged to have his heart recreated and his hands purified. He pleaded for compassion, and God heard him. David's story is a powerful reminder that God responds to honesty and repentance with mercy and forgiveness.

God, cleanse me from my sin and create a new heart within me. Restore the joy of your salvation to my heart.

Scripture Reading: Psalms 53-56

Cast Your Cares

Cast your cares on the Lord
and he will sustain you;
he will never let
the righteous be shaken.
Psalm 55:22 NIV

In Psalm 55, David seems to have been betrayed by a close friend. This friend has been spreading lies and damaging David's reputation. As a result, David feels like there is a battle raging against him. He is overwhelmed by the trouble he is in, but he has a source of strength that his enemies can't comprehend.

The hurt David received from his friend could not overpower the confidence he received from God. David believed that God was too faithful and too mighty to be overcome by deception. He knew that God would get him through this uncomfortable season. From that place of dependence David declares that he will cast his cares upon God. He fully trusted that God would take care of him.

Heavenly Father, my burdens and hurts pale in comparison to your greatness and faithfulness. Take my cares today and help me trust in you.

Scripture Reading: Psalms 57-60

Confident in the Cave

Your steadfast love is great to the heavens,
your faithfulness to the clouds.
PSALM 57:10 ESV

David had confidence that he was safe in God's hands even when he was hiding from Saul in a cave. His unwavering trust didn't make sense to anyone around him. In their view, David had every reason to be afraid, frustrated, and vengeful. They thought David was justified to act like Saul and sink to his level of hostility and violence.

David chose a better path by trusting God. David found tremendous hope and freedom in the darkest circumstances. He didn't waver even when it seemed like there was no way out. David stood firm in the unrelenting love of God instead of fighting with the same weapons as his enemies. He had full assurance that God would intervene on his behalf.

God, empower me today with the greatness of your steadfast love. Don't let the distractions of my burdens darken my heart.

Scripture Reading: Psalms 61-64

Faith like David

Let all that I am wait quietly before God,
for my hope is in him.
Psalm 62:5 NLT

David consistently modeled unwavering trust in God during crushing circumstances. The psalms he penned carry the consistent theme of leaning on the Lord even when it doesn't make sense. David chose quietness of heart when he was surrounded by chaos. He didn't let his circumstances dictate the state of his soul. Instead, he lifted his eyes above his physical troubles and focused on the steadfast nature of the Lord.

David's faith is an encouragement to all of us. We can look at his example and also choose to trust that God will help us overcome whatever troubles we face. He will rescue us and keep us safe. He will lead us toward eternal life when we put our trust in him. We can find courage in David's words and put our full confidence in the Lord as well.

Heavenly Father, I place my hope in you and your plans for my life.

Scripture Reading: Psalms 65-68

Kind Father

A father of the fatherless and a judge for the widows,
Is God in His holy dwelling.

Psalm 68:5 NASB

God cares for those who are broken, and he comforts those who are hurting. God bends down to pick up those who have fallen, and he has compassion for those who feel they've been cast aside. He notices the overlooked, and he invites everyone to join him at his table. He is a father to the fatherless, and he is a safe haven for those who are grieving and suffering.

Offering our lives to the Lord is the best decision we could ever make. We lay our lives down because he is worthy, and we put our confidence in him because he is kind. We are not his servants or his lowly admirers; we are his beloved children. He looks at us with great compassion and pride. He longs to lift us up, heal our brokenness, and make us whole.

Lord, you are wonderful. Your love does not fail. Your care does not waver. You are so good.

Scripture Reading: Psalms 69-72

Floodwaters of Life

Don't let the floodwaters sweep over me
or the deep swallow me up;
don't let the Pit close its mouth over me.
PSALM 69:15 CSB

As David wrote this psalm, he felt like he was drowning in a sea of hostility. There were numerous people who hated him and sought to destroy him. He was overwhelmed by his own sin, and even his closest brothers rejected him. He was the subject of gossip in his hometown, and he could not rely on anyone to rescue him.

David knew that he could rely on God. He knew he needed God to show up, or he wouldn't survive. He knew that there wasn't a person on earth who could deliver him trouble or protect him from his enemies. He entrusted God with his heart and declared him the keeper of his soul. He put his life in his hands, knowing that there was no safer place for him to be.

Lord, only you can get me out of the overwhelming messes I face. Help me depend on you in every circumstance.

Scripture Reading: Psalms 73-76

Raw Honesty

My flesh and my heart may fail,
but God is the strength of my heart
and my portion forever.
PSALM 73:26 NIV

Psalm 73 contains some of the darkest laments in the Bible. The psalmist expresses deep pain and despair. It is sometimes shocking in its honest, raw misery. The psalmist's pain is vividly depicted, yet he never loses sight of the fact that God is ultimately in control. There is a clear recognition of God's trustworthy nature.

Psalm 73 seems to have been deliberately chosen as the first psalm in this section because it effectively establishes these themes. It gives words to someone who is struggling yet knows that their hope is in God. The Psalms give credence to the very real struggle between hope and the recognition of reality. They are refreshing because they remind us that there is no struggle that has not already been faced by someone in history.

God, thank you for the encouragement found in the book of Psalms. May my prayers be as honest and raw as those.

Scripture Reading: Psalms 77-80

Each Generation

Each generation should set its hope anew on God,
not forgetting his glorious miracles
and obeying his commands.
PSALM 78:7 NLT

Psalm 78 is a very long chapter. Most of its seventy-two verses walk through the history of Israel's relationship with God. Most of the relationship is marked by Israel's unfaithfulness. God's people repeatedly failed to model a resilient faith that could be passed on to the next generation.

While Psalm 78 paints an overwhelmingly sad picture of what happens when a generation fails to follow God, it also gives an inspiring account of determination. The writer declares that this current generation will be different. This generation, he says, will intentionally leave a legacy of faith that will impact those to come. Psalm 78 is a reminder that patterns can be changed, and new habits can be formed.

Lord, may I be a part of a generation that empowers the next to live for you. May my actions and words honor you.

Scripture Reading: Psalms 81-84

Cry For Justice

"Give justice to the weak and the fatherless;
maintain the right of the afflicted and the destitute.
Rescue the weak and the needy;
deliver them from the hand of the wicked."

PSALM 82:3-4 ESV

There are people in this world who cause tremendous suffering. They wage war on families and communities. They leave people orphaned. They thrive on oppression and an unequal balance of power. They spread chaos and harm, forcing people to scatter in search of food and shelter. Such people are wicked and are enemies of God's plan for this earth.

The writer of Psalm 82 is fed up by the movement of the wicked, so he cries out to God for justice to be done. He questions how long the wicked will be able to continue getting away with these things. His prayers are a reminder that we can petition God in the same way. When we see injustice, we can call upon the Lord to make things right.

Lord, break my heart for those who are suffering at the hands of evil people in this world. Stir me to cry out to you about it.

Scripture Reading: Psalms 85-88

Close Relationship

Bend down, O Lord, and hear my prayer;
answer me, for I need your help.
Psalm 86:1 NLT

David was a man among men. He killed a lion and bear to protect his sheep, and he slew a giant in before thousands of enemy soldiers. He led a rabble of hundreds of dubious men for years through caves and hostile territories. He commanded armies and established a peaceful kingdom. He was as stereotypically masculine as it gets.

David also deeply loved the Lord. The intimacy of David's relationship with God is an intriguing example for us. His devotion and praise was full of emotion and vulnerability. He had the courage to be authentic and open before God. He wasn't afraid to let his emotions be seen.

Jesus, draw me closer to you today. Help me embrace my weakness before you and offer you my unhindered devotion.

July

**In the beginning was the Word,
and the Word was with God,
and the Word was God.**

John 1:1 CSB

Scripture Reading: Psalms 89-92

Heaven and Earth

I will declare that your love stands firm forever,
that you have established your faithfulness in heaven itself.
PSALM 89:2 NIV

When Jesus instructs his disciples to pray he encourages them to acknowledge that heaven already has what earth needs. Heaven has peace; earth needs peace. Heaven has no sickness, disease, or shortage of life; earth needs a daily supply of healing and hope. Heaven has no sin; earth needs to be forgiven of sin and rescued from temptation.

In his wisdom, the writer of Psalm 89 knew that earth needs God's kingdom to come. He knew that God's reign was awe-inspiring and perfectly good. He knew God ruled with unfailing love and eternal salvation. He saw firsthand glimpses of God's eternal reign as David and Solomon established the kingdom of Israel in Jerusalem, so he made it the goal of his life to declare the greatness of God's kingdom on this earth.

Lord, may your kingdom come on earth as it is in heaven. May your reign be established in my life today.

Scripture Reading: Psalms 93-96

Standing on the Rock

Mightier than the thunder of the great waters,
mightier than the breakers of the sea—
the LORD on high is mighty.
PSALM 93:4 NIV

A lighthouse is built on indestructible rock. It is built firmly on a solid foundation, enabling it to shine a beacon of safety in the darkest of storms. Winds and waves may thunder against it, but a lighthouse is built to withstand the onslaught of the worst seasons.

That idea echoes the imagery of Psalm 93. The Lord's throne has been established on the firmament of the earth. Darkness and chaos rise up on the earth, but the Lord is high and mighty. He will not be shaken or disturbed. He provides safety and guidance for all who look to him. He is mightier than the thunder of the great waters, and he will not be removed from his throne.

Lord, I will build my house on your rock. I will seek you for guidance in the midst of any storm. You alone are my refuge and strength.

Scripture Reading: Psalms 97-100

Unfailing Love

The LORD is good.
His unfailing love continues forever,
and his faithfulness continues to each generation.
PSALM 100:5 NLT

There is so much to celebrate! There is so much to be glad about. Let us gather and worship the Lord with great joy! He is worthy of our praise, and we are most satisfied when we delight in him. He is our God, and we are his people. We were created to live in his presence, and we are blessed by his faithfulness.

There is no one like the Lord. We are the sheep of his pasture, and he is our Good Shepherd. He tends to us with great care and attentiveness. He is kind, merciful, powerful, and mighty. We can enter his gates with thanksgiving because he has done wonderful things for us. His faithfulness continues to each generation. There will never be a generation that does not know his faithful, unfailing love.

O Lord, you are good! Your love is unfailing, and your faithfulness is unstoppable. I praise you today!

Scripture Reading: Psalms 101-104

Bless the Lord

Bless the LORD, my soul,
And all that is within me, bless His holy name.
Bless the LORD, my soul,
And do not forget any of His benefits.
PSALM 103:1-2 NASB

Each of us could write an unending list testifying of God's goodness. He has faithfully intervened on behalf of his people for all of time, and he won't stop now. Reminding ourselves of his goodness allows us to offer him a continual offering of praise. When we struggle to remember what he's done, we can open up the book of Psalms for inspiration.

Psalm 103 reassures us that the Lord does good things for us! He forgives my sins, and he heals our diseases. He redeems us from death, and he crowns us with love. He fills our lives with good things and renews our strength. He gives justice to those who have been treated badly. He is compassionate and merciful. He is slow to anger and abounding in love.

God, may I sing your praises all through the day. Don't let me forget all you have done for me.

Scripture Reading: Psalms 105-108

Speaking Out

Has the LORD redeemed you? Then speak out!
Tell others he has redeemed you from your enemies.
PSALM 107:2 NLT

This psalm urges those who have been redeemed by God to speak out. It urges the reader to remember the practical things God has done. It's a reminder that there is strength found in testifying of God's good work. We are encouraged when we tell the people around us what God has done for us.

God has redeemed us, and he is worthy of our praise. When we share our testimonies, we encourage both ourselves and others. It is good to publicly declare the miracles we have witnessed.

Lord, thank you for redeeming me! Help me look for opportunities to speak out about all you have done.

Scripture Reading: Psalms 109-112

Time of Need

With my mouth I will greatly extol the LORD;
in the great throng of worshipers I will praise him.
For he stands at the right hand of the needy,
to save their lives from those who would condemn them.

PSALM 109:30-31 NIV

David wrote this psalm out of a sense of anxiety. He was being slandered by his enemies. People were threatening to remove him from his position and turn his family into beggars. They sought to seize his estate and wished publicly that his family would be ruined. As a result, David's heart had been broken.

He called upon the Lord in his time of distress. He had already experienced God's goodness, and he knew that God would rescue him. He was confident that God would stand with him in his difficult situation. It's important to remember that we can do the same thing. If we are convinced of God's faithfulness, we won't hesitate to bring him our needs.

Lord, give me the courage to cry out to you when I am being attacked by others. Help me place my trust in you for salvation.

Scripture Reading: Psalms 113-115

Not to Us

Not to us, O LORD, not to us, but to your name give glory, for the sake of your steadfast love and your faithfulness!

PSALM 115:1 ESV

All glory belongs to God. To seek glory for ourselves is to steal from God what is rightfully his. He is the reason for every good gift we have. He is the source of every blessing. He created us, and he sustains us. Giving him the credit he is due is simply an acknowledgement of reality.

We were created to worship. If we do not worship the one true God, we will turn our attention to someone or something else. It's inevitable. We were created to admire, adore, and praise the one who made us. We find belonging in his presence and satisfaction as we follow his ways.

God, my life is meant for your glory. Forgive me for seeking to glorify myself.

Scripture Reading: Psalms 116-118

This Is the Day

This is the day the LORD has made;
let's rejoice and be glad in it.
PSALM 118:24 CSB

Psalm 118 contains immense comfort for those who need to be reminded of God's faithfulness. The repeated refrain that God's love endures forever fills us with confidence despite our circumstances. It's a reminder that God's love is eternally reliable no matter what is happening in our daily lives. We can depend on God to see us through whatever we are facing because we are precious to him, and he won't give up on us.

God has made today. He is the author of time, and he holds it securely in his hands. He knows exactly what each day will contain, and we can trust his ability to orchestrate every part of our story. It's not our job to micromanage our time; it's our job to grasp ahold of each opportunity to seek the Lord and rejoice in what he has done.

Lord, you made this day, and I am glad. Let me rejoice throughout the day for the opportunity I have to praise you and proclaim the greatness of your name.

Scripture Reading: Psalm 119

Hidden Word

I have hidden your word in my heart,
that I might not sin against you.
PSALM 119:11 NLT

Psalm 119 is easily the longest chapter in the Bible. Tremendous attention was given to writing this psalm. It is divided into twenty-two acrostic sections based on the Hebrew alphabet. Each section poetically begins with the letter represented by that section, and the entirety of this psalm focuses on God's Word and commands.

The writer of Psalm 119 loves God's Word. He delights in it, and he is refreshed by it. He patterns his life according to God's commands, and he trusts the reliability of God's instructions. He finds guidance in the Word of God, and he knows that he will never exhaust the depth of its wisdom. He finds the power he needs to avoid making sinful mistakes by embedding the Word of God into his heart. The Word provides him with everything he needs to live a blessed life.

Lord, may your Word resound in my soul today. Help me hide truth in my heart and honor you in all I do.

Scripture Reading: Psalms 120-123

Source of Help

I lift up my eyes to the mountains—
where does my help come from?
My help comes from the Lord,
the Maker of heaven and earth.

Psalm 121:1-2 NIV

This psalm promises that God will not let us stumble. He does not sleep as he watches over our lives. Our help comes from him, the Maker of heaven and earth. He offers us protection from harm by shielding us with his mercy. He creates peace in the midst of hostility and order in the midst of chaos.

God's promised protection does not mean we won't have trouble. We know that the world is filled with liars and deceitful people who cause suffering and hostility. We also know that sometimes we experience the consequences of our own actions. Psalm 121 is our reassurance that God is our ever-present source of help no matter what we are experiencing.

Lord, I look to you for help. Empower me today to stand boldly in the face of struggle.

Scripture Reading: Psalms 124-127

God's Work

It is useless for you to work so hard
from early morning until late at night,
anxiously working for food to eat;
for God gives rest to his loved ones.
Psalm 127:2 NLT

If we want our work to have a lasting impact, we must build upon a firm foundation. If we want our plans to have eternal value, we must surrender them to the Lord. God's involvement determines the success of our days. If we sweat and toil apart from him, we are not actually accomplishing anything.

Working faithfully within the will of God is not as complicated as we make it. He has given responsibilities to each of us. If we have wives, we should seek to honor the Lord in how we treat them. If we have children, we should seek to be a Father who pleases God. We don't need to go looking for great and glorious things to do when God has already given us something to focus on.

Lord, don't let me waste my time or efforts. Help me focus my energy on things you care about.

Scripture Reading: Psalms 128-131

Forgiven and Free

If You, LORD, were to keep account of guilty deeds,
LORD, who could stand?
But there is forgiveness with You,
So that You may be revered.

PSALM 130:3 NASB

The Lord offers forgiveness to those who follow him. He does not want anyone to perish under the weight of sin. He did not create us to be defeated or separated from him. He created us to be free and to flourish in relationship with him for all eternity.

God wants to redeem us from our guilt. He longs for us to experience the freedom and joy that he offers. We are mistaken if we see him as a tyrant or an irritated rule enforcer. His heart toward us is kind and generous. He is delighted when we offer him our sins, and he is delighted by forgiving them. Trusting him with our sins is an incredible act of worship because it is an acknowledgment that he alone is capable of forgiving us and showing mercy.

God, I am counting on you for the forgiveness of my sin! Thank you for sending Jesus as my Savior to take away my guilt.

Scripture Reading: Psalms 132-135

Blessing of Unity

How good and pleasant it is
when God's people live together in unity!
Psalm 133:1 NIV

Mount Hermon is a 9,000-foot-tall snow-capped mountain in Syria and northern Lebanon. In the Bible it is considered the northern border of Solomon's kingdom. It contains the source of much of the fresh water that forms the Jordan River and the Sea of Galilee. The moisture from Mount Hermon often creates dew that provides water for much of the dry wilderness around northern Israel.

In Psalm 133 David compares the refreshing impact of the water from Mount Hermon to the blessing experienced by people who have harmony with one another. The concept of harmony appealed greatly to David. He had experienced so much betrayal and hatred during his lifetime that the idea of peace revived his soul. He knew firsthand that working together to accomplish God's plans was beautiful and pleasing to the Lord.

Lord, help me live in harmony with those around me. Give me brothers who are like-minded in faith and who encourage me to live for you.

Scripture Reading: Psalms 136-139

Confidence and Connection

The LORD will fulfill his purpose for me;
your steadfast love, O LORD, endures forever.
Do not forsake the work of your hands.
PSALM 138:8 ESV

David trusted the Lord with the outcomes of his life more than he trusted himself. David knew that he had shortcomings and weaknesses, but he also knew that God had made promises to establish his kingdom through David. He trusted God's ability to fulfill his plans and purposes. He had confidence in God's faithfulness.

We can learn from David's confidence and connection. Our ability to rely on God's promises comes directly from our willingness to abide in him. We won't trust his Word if we never spend time with him. We won't believe what he says if we don't experience his steadfast love on a daily basis. When we seek him with all our hearts like David, we will also develop an unwavering confidence in his promises.

Lord, I trust you for the outcomes of my life. Help me stay close to you as I follow your commands.

Scripture Reading: Psalms 140-143

Each Morning

Let me hear of your unfailing love each morning,
for I am trusting you.
Show me where to walk,
for I give myself to you.
Psalm 143:8 NLT

The reason for this devotional book is to spend time in the Word of God every single day. By doing so, we grow closer to him and cultivate strong character. God's Word helps us learn to better reflect his love to others. It helps us stay faithful to God's calling, and it helps us honor him in all we do.

It is for this reason that David wrote Psalm 143. He prayed that God would teach him to do his will. He wanted God's Spirit to direct his steps and keep him from falling. David wanted to be empowered to face the difficult circumstances in his life, and he knew that spending time with the Lord was the only way to do that. He knew that a daily walk with God was what gave him the strength to go on.

Heavenly Father, thank you for meeting with me each morning. Thank you for equipping me for my day and strengthening me by your Spirit.

Scripture Reading: Psalms 144-147

Human Experience

The LORD is gracious and compassionate,
slow to anger and great in faithful love.
PSALM 145:8 CSB

Through the book of Psalms David cannot contain what he has come to know about God. He is constantly declaring various truths about who God is. His words are poetic, thankful, and full of passion. He provides the reader with a multitude of examples of how to glorify the Lord through word and song.

The verses that David penned offer us a glimpse into the reality of human experience. We see the full spectrum of emotions being offered to the Lord. There is no shame in giving him our grief, joy, frustration, excitement, and doubt. Like David, we can give God whatever happens to be within our hearts at any moment. As we look toward him in every circumstance, he softens our hearts and draws us closer to him in worship. Like David, we can offer God the reality of our experience and expect that he will respond with patience and compassion.

Lord, you are so good. Thank you for taking my burdens and responding to me in love.

Scripture Reading: Psalms 148-150

Praise the Lord

Let everything that has breath praise the LORD.
Praise the LORD.

PSALM 150:6 NIV

Scripture teaches us that everything was created by God, he holds all of creation together, and everything was made to bring glory to him forever. If the chief aim of mankind is to bring glory to God, it is very appropriate for the final psalm to be filled with unrestrained praise. The crescendo of this book is the glorification of the Lord!

Praise the Lord! Praise the Lord for the incredible things he has done. Praise him for being so much greater than anything or anyone else. We owe everything we have to him. He fills our lungs with breath, and we offer it back to him through worship. He keeps our footsteps steady, and in response we walk along the path he has chosen for us.

Lord, I praise you right now. Prompt me to praise you all day long and in every circumstance.

Scripture Reading: Proverbs 1-3

Entrust Your Steps

Trust in the LORD with all your heart,
and do not lean on your own understanding.
In all your ways acknowledge him,
and he will make straight your paths.
PROVERBS 3:5-6 ESV

When we seek the Lord's direction for our lives, he smooths crooked paths and maps out a productive course. When we trust ourselves more than God, we inevitably get caught up in a twisted maze. It is better to stay committed to God's ways than to trust in our own abilities. His plans are always better than ours.

It's good to take time for self-evaluation. We show that we are wise when we are willing to adjust our path. Everyone wanders off course at some point, and it takes humility to acknowledge that we need to make changes. The good news is that God is always eager and willing to help. He loves it when we ask him for direction, and he is happy to show us where to go.

Lord, take captive my thoughts and behaviors. Help me entrust the next steps of my life to you. May my life be glorifying to you alone.

Scripture Reading: Proverbs 4-6

Hold On

Hold on to instruction; don't let go.
Guard it, for it is your life.
Keep off the path of the wicked;
don't proceed on the way of evil ones.
Avoid it; don't travel on it.
Turn away from it, and pass it by.
PROVERBS 4:13-15 CSB

There is no stumbling for the one who walks according to the wisdom of God. In contrast, we forfeit God's protection when we refuse to follow his ways. He promises to equip us and keep us from falling, but we must be devoted to his promises and purposes.

Avoiding the path of the wicked requires awareness. We must be able to see the enemy's schemes for what they are. It's much easier to flee from temptation when we are not blinded to our own weaknesses. In order to see ourselves clearly, we must follow the guidance of the Holy Spirit. He is capable of guiding us through the plights of the world and our own misconceptions.

Heavenly Father, help me walk on the path of wisdom and remain faithful to your truth. Give me deep conviction for your standards and commands.

Scripture Reading: Proverbs 7-9

Wisdom's Voice

"Stolen water is refreshing;
food eaten in secret tastes the best!"
But little do they know that the dead are there.
Her guests are in the depths of the grave.
PROVERBS 9:17-18 NLT

The book of Proverbs repeatedly presents stark contrasts. It reminds us that our perception of what is good isn't always in alignment with the Lord's. There will be times in life when something looks valuable, satisfying, and delightful, but the truth is that it will cause turmoil and chaos in our lives.

While there are plenty of opportunities for temptation to flourish, there is another voice that calls out to us. Proverbs teaches that wisdom speaks to us, and her voice is beautiful, pure, and good. Wisdom urges us to remain committed and true in all circumstances. Wisdom reminds us of the eternal value of following God's ways.

Lord, keep my focus pure. Fill my mind with your Word so that there is no room for temptation.

Scripture Reading: Proverbs 10-12

Accept Discipline

People who accept discipline are on the pathway to life,
but those who ignore correction will go astray.
PROVERBS 10:17 NLT

Accepting discipline shows maturity and wisdom. Being unable to accept discipline shows that we are either prideful or ignorant to the truth of God's character. God disciplines those he loves, and we can trust that his discipline is always in our best interest. If we are convinced we can do everything alone or we view God as harsh or authoritative, we won't accept his correction or guidance.

How can we accept discipline and correction? There are many practical ways to embrace teachability. We can refrain from giving excuses when our flaws are uncovered. We can calmly apologize rather than defending ourselves. We can look at our own hearts instead of shifting blame to the people around us. Discipline might feel painful, but it leads to life.

Lord, help me embrace growth and change. Soften my heart and teach me how to accept discipline.

Scripture Reading: Proverbs 13-15

Think First

Someone with a quick temper does foolish things,
but someone with understanding remains calm.
PROVERBS 14:17 NCV

Our society is filled with people who don't think before they speak. Hot-headed hostility and empty debates cause division and strife. Communities crumble under the weight of pride, while our culture seems to feed off of the loudest and most brash voices. Flashes of foolishness is fraying our communities.

Those who wait to speak are a refreshing contrast to the aggressive urgencies of the day. The ability to maintain composure and embrace understanding creates peace. Fiery arguments and pointed comments might garner applause, but discernment and thoughtful answers generates peace and respect. We are wise when we pause and reflect on a situation before responding.

Lord, help me think before I react to the quick-tempered foolishness of our world. Teach me how to be patient and thoughtful.

Scripture Reading: Proverbs 16-18

Committed to God

Commit your work to the LORD,
and your plans will be established.
PROVERBS 16:3 ESV

The logic is simple. If we try to accomplish something that fits into God's plan, it will be successful. If we try to accomplish something that goes against God's plan, we are going to have a difficult time getting it done. After all, everything is meant for the glory of God. Therefore, it is good to ask whether the work we are doing brings glory to God.

Why labor in vain when we could devote ourselves to the established plans of the Lord? Why not seek the Lord's blessing on the work ahead? We can trust his guidance with our whole hearts. We can take each step with confidence because we know he won't lead us astray. Following him isn't always easy, but it is always worth it.

God, I don't want to labor in vain today. May your will be done in all that I do.

Scripture Reading: Proverbs 19-21

Finish the Job

Lazy people take food in their hand
but don't even lift it to their mouth.
PROVERBS 19:24 NLT

How often do we make dinner and leave the dishes in the sink or do the laundry and leave it in the basket? How often do we remodel a room and leave the trim unfished for months? The last step is often the hardest. It is not abnormal for people to get 90% of their work done and then lose motivation. Those final moments of effort and those last annoying details are problematic for people who don't want to work anymore. It takes discipline to finish a job in entirety.

Laziness is much bigger problem than most people realize. It seems harmless because we aren't really doing anything to hurt anyone. At the same time, we can clearly see that God values hard work. Proverbs is filled with admonitions to embrace excellence and take pride in whatever we put our hands to. Each job we tackle is an opportunity to worship the Lord with our attitude and work ethic.

Lord, help me accomplish what you have called me to do. Give me grace to tackle what you've put in front of me with courage and excellence.

Scripture Reading: Proverbs 22-24

God's Priorities

Don't wear yourself out trying to get rich.
Be wise enough to know when to quit.
In the blink of an eye wealth disappears,
for it will sprout wings
and fly away like an eagle.

PROVERBS 23:4-5 NLT

Some of us will spend our lives wondering what it's like to have zero financial stress. Others must make deliberate decisions to stop accumulating wealth. Our circumstances matter less than our ability to navigate our finances with humility and wisdom. If we want to follow the Lord, we must be willing to surrender our finances to him.

We all know we need money to live, but we must ask ourselves if our priorities are aligned with God's. Do we trust God for provision, or do we frantically search for more? Do we hold our money with an open grasp, or do we stockpile it for ourselves? Do we practice generosity and humility, or do we feel secure only if we see certain numbers on our balance sheet?

Lord, help me honor you with my money. Align my heart with yours and show me opportunities to be generous. Help me trust you for the provision above all else.

Scripture Reading: Proverbs 25-27

Good Friends

As iron sharpens iron,
So one person sharpens another.
PROVERBS 27:17 NASB

A man needs someone who will motivate him to become the best version of himself. Like a weight-lifting partner in the gym, a man needs someone who will motivate him to work hard and develop self-discipline. A man needs someone who believes he has something to accomplish and who is committed to helping him remain focused on his calling. A man needs someone who is not afraid to sharpen him into the man God created him to be.

A man without such a friend is a man likely to fall into decay. A man without a coach has no one to hold him accountable to healthy practices and responsible behavior. A man without a mentor has no one to challenge him to set goals and implement beneficial daily habits. A man without a friend has no one to encourage him to deepen his faith in God.

God, surround me with men of faith who will challenge me to grow as a man of integrity and strength.

Scripture Reading: Proverbs 28-29

Avoid Flattery

A person who flatters his neighbor
spreads a net for his feet.
PROVERBS 29:5 CSB

Flattery cannot be trusted. Embellished compliments and flowing praises hide a trap. The person who spews flattery uses manipulation to get what they want. They make people feel noticed or loved, but they have hidden motivations. They are more worried about their own selfish gain than actually encouraging others.

Flattery is especially dangerous for those who feel insecure. This is why it is so important for our identity to be firmly rooted in the Lord. We are less prone to persuasion when we are confident that his opinion is the only one that matters. His perspective is perfect and trustworthy, and he is the one we should look to for validation.

Heavenly Father, give me the courage to seek honesty over empty praise.

Scripture Reading: Proverbs 30-31

The Answer

Who has gone up to heaven and come down?
Whose hands have gathered up the wind?
Who has wrapped up the waters in a cloak?
Who has established all the ends of the earth?
What is his name, and what is the name of his son?
Surely you know!

PROVERBS 30:4 NIV

Who can cleanse us of our sin? Who can calm the storms in our life? Who can speak truth that cuts through the fog of culture? Who has created the earth with his voice? Who has taken on flesh so God could be with us? Who has carried the cross for the forgiveness of sin? Who has gone to the grave and come back out?

Jesus is the answer to everything we seek. He is our Wonderful Counselor and our Almighty God. He is our Prince of Peace and the Lion of Judah. He is the Lamb of God and the Good Shepherd whom we trust implicitly. Our recognition of who he is and our devotion to his ways is what sets us free. He alone is worthy of everything we have to give.

Jesus, my Savior and Lord, you are the answer to the deepest longings of my soul. Fill me with a greater sense of devotion.

Scripture Reading: Ecclesiastes 1-4

Chasing the Wind

I considered all my activities which my hands had done and the labor which I had exerted, and behold, all was futility and striving after wind, and there was no benefit under the sun.

ECCLESIASTES 2:11 NASB

Solomon accumulated great wealth, yet it couldn't bring him lasting contentment. He achieved unthinkable fame, yet it didn't give him security or confidence. He was known for his incredible wisdom, yet even that didn't give him gratification. He had everything he ever wanted, and he still acknowledged the Lord as the one who satisfies the soul. He saw through the emptiness of worldly treasures and recognized that life is meaningless without God.

Life is fragile, and we are not meant to desperately hunt for our own satisfaction. Searching for our own happiness is like chasing the wind. Our time on earth is fleeting, and our time spent in eternity vastly outweighs our time here. This is why our greatest hope must be found in Jesus. We will only be satisfied if we keep our eyes on him and all that he offers us.

Lord, you give my life true meaning. Keep me safe from the temptation to chase worldly treasures.

Scripture Reading: Ecclesiastes 5-8

Never Satisfied

Whoever loves money never has enough;
whoever loves wealth is never satisfied with their income.
This too is meaningless.

ECCLESIASTES 5:10 NIV

The book of Ecclesiastes provides a blunt reminder to us about what is not important in life. Solomon is very clear, and he does not hold back. Money is not worth the effort because it never satisfies. Money promises fulfillment, but it leaves people empty. The happiness that it provides is fleeting, and the goal post is always moving.

Solomon watched money ruin people. He watched wealthy people succumb to worry and anxiety because they were always worried about losing their treasures. He warns us against giving all our time and energy to the pursuit of money. He soberly urges us to remember that we cannot take any of our money to the grave.

Lord, free me from the love of money. Lead me along your path and help me be generous and wise with the financial blessings you've given me.

Scripture Reading: Ecclesiastes 9-12

Final Conclusion

That's the whole story. Here now is my final conclusion: Fear God and obey his commands, for this is everyone's duty.

ECCLESIASTES 12:13 NLT

At the end of Ecclesiastes Solomon concludes that man is only satisfied by the presence of God. He sums up his lifetime of wisdom, riches, and recognition by saying that the only thing that really matters is fearing God and obeying his commands. He had learned that nothing else could bring contentment to his heart. He had access to everything under the sun, yet he knew that God was better than all of it.

Solomon didn't just assume that God was worth pursuing. He spent his life proving it. He chased after worldly treasures, and he attained them. He wasn't lacking in anything. He was dissatisfied despite having everything he ever wished for. We tend to fall into the same trap. How often do we think everything will be better if we just have more money, a different job, or that one material item? Let's learn from Solomon and remember that the fear of the Lord is the only means of true fulfillment.

Lord, keep me from temporary enticements that lead me astray. Give me grace to keep my eyes on you no matter what temptations come my way.

August

Every word of God is pure;
he is a shield to those who take
refuge in him.

Proverbs 30:5 csb

Scripture Reading: Song of Solomon 1-4

Unapologetic Affection

The Song of Songs, which is Solomon's.
SONG OF SONGS 1:1 CSB

The Song of Songs is an unashamed, uncensored love story. It has stood the test of time as a testimony to what it means for a man to adore his bride and for a woman to desire her husband. It's poetic and unapologetic as it describes God's design for marriage. The relationship outlined by Solomon is defined by care, commitment, passion, and delight.

Ultimately, the Song of Songs also serves as parable for the affection that Jesus has for the Church. In Scripture he is called the Bridegroom, and we are the bride. Song of Solomon provides a significant picture of the sort of desire we should have for God on a daily basis. It illustrates the idea that God's love is faithful and strong through every circumstance.

Jesus, help me understand your love for your people. Thank you for being so devoted to us.

Scripture Reading: Song of Solomon 5-8

Wholly Committed

"I am my beloved's and my beloved is mine,
He who pastures his flock among the lilies."
SONG OF SONGS 6:3 NASB

Today's Scripture is the crescendo of the entire book. The bride declares her commitment with joy. She has eyes for only one person. The idea of unfaithfulness or adultery doesn't cloud her thinking. Her heart for her husband is so innocent and pure that she is wholly focused on him. There are no doubts or distractions. She knows that she belongs to the one who loves her, and he belongs to her.

This is an example of the kind of assurance that is available to anyone who believes in Jesus. We can completely trust that Jesus is committed to us and that he loves us with deep affection. We can also know that as the Holy Spirit works to sanctify us and recreate us. We can rediscover the sort of innocent faith that knows without a doubt that Jesus is all we would ever need.

Lord, keep me from being distracted and help me focus on you. Thank you for reminding me of your steady commitment to me.

Scripture Reading: Isaiah 1-4

Hope-filled Prophecies

"Learn to do right; seek justice.
Defend the oppressed.
Take up the cause of the fatherless;
plead the case of the widow."

ISAIAH 1:17 NIV

There is so much hope mixed into the Book of Isaiah. This massive collection of prophecies is packed with God's promises about his plan of redemption. Isaiah points to a Messiah who walk the earth, suffer for our sins, and rise from the dead to offer us eternal healing.

Isaiah himself served as a messenger for God during a very interesting time in Judah. He advised and regularly confronted four different kings. The first few chapters of the book depict a confrontation. Isaiah gives a message from God to the people. He urges them to repent from their sins and walk with God. He calls them to a higher standard and reminds them of what matters to God.

Lord, forgive me for not walking according to your ways. Help me reflect your holiness.

Scripture Reading: Isaiah 5-8

Send Me

Then I heard the LORD asking, "Whom should I send as a messenger to this people? Who will go for us?" I said, "Here I am. Send me."

ISAIAH 6:8 NLT

God was looking for someone who would stand up for him against the nations the wayward kings of Judah. Isaiah certainly didn't feel worthy. He didn't feel like he should even be able to stand in God's presence. He felt unqualified, but the Lord commissioned him despite his flaws. The Lord removed his guilt and forgave his sin.

Like Isaiah, we each have a calling to represent God wherever he sends us. We are his messengers, and our goal is to show the world who he is and how much he loves his people. He wants us to care for those who are lost, overlooked, and mistreated. He wants us to share his love with those who have hardened their hearts, plugged their ears, and closed their eyes toward his goodness. He wants us to share his good news with people who need to return to him.

Lord, I am not worthy, but I am willing. If you empower me, I will go.

Scripture Reading: Isaiah 9-12

The Coming Messiah

To us a child is born,
to us a son is given;
and the government shall be upon his shoulder,
and his name shall be called
Wonderful Counselor, Mighty God,
Everlasting Father, Prince of Peace.

Isaiah 9:6 ESV

Jesus' life, death, and resurrection are predicted and foreshadowed throughout the book of Isaiah. In chapter 7, Isaiah suggests that the Messiah would be born to a virgin and would be called Immanuel which means "God with us." This would have been revolutionary at the time. The idea that God himself would walk among his people would have been shocking.

We serve a God who came down from his place on high, willingly suffered on our behalf, and offers us his faithful companionship for all our days. He is personal, kind, and attentive. He pursues us out of love and devotion, and he offers us incredible freedom. He is unlike any other god that has ever been worshipped in all of history. He is perfect in all his ways, and he is worthy of all our praise.

God, thank you for sending your Son to save me.

Scripture Reading: Isaiah 13-16

All Nations

"The LORD Almighty has purposed,
and who can thwart him?
His hand is stretched out,
and who can turn it back?"

ISAIAH 14:27 NIV

Though God's people wandered for a long time, he would not allow them to remain scattered forever. Though they had been exiled to Babylon, the Lord would gather them back in Jerusalem. Isaiah clearly articulated to the surrounding kings that this was the Lord's plan. He would redeem his people, and they would belong to him.

When God prophesied redemption, he wasn't just referring to Israel and Judah. He calls all people back to him. He stretches his hand over all nations and declares that we are his people. He is the King of Kings and the Lord Almighty. He is sovereign over all the earth, and each person was created in his image. We all belong in his eternal kingdom.

Lord, restore your reign fully on this earth. Bring all nations under your care.

Scripture Reading: Isaiah 17-20

Through the Mundane

Then at last the people will look to their Creator
and turn their eyes to the Holy One of Israel.

Isaiah 17:7 NLT

Part of the purpose of the exile was to remind God's people to look to him for salvation. They rejected him, but he did not reject them. They had broken their covenant vow, but he did not break his. He did, however, want to nudge them to remember him. The exile was like a defibrillator, jump starting Israel's heart.

Sometimes it takes difficult circumstances for us to remember the goodness of God. It's almost easier to surrender to him when we feel desperate or overwhelmed. Let's strive to be people who devote our lives to him on a daily basis. We don't need to wait for everything to implode before we call upon his name. He longs to walk with us through the mundane details of our lives. Let's offer him what we have right now.

Lord, keep my gaze fixed on you. Help me stay devoted to you through every high, low, and in between moment.

Scripture Reading: Isaiah 21-24

The Wages of Sin

The earth is polluted by its inhabitants,
for they have transgressed teachings,
overstepped decrees,
and broken the permanent covenant.

Isaiah 24:5 csb

The prophecies of devastation in Isaiah are alarming. It is difficult for many modern readers to make sense of the wrath God. It feels uncomfortable to reconcile the goodness of God with the consequences of sin. Many of us don't immediately consider that Israel and Judah had been rejecting the Lord for hundreds of years. It's easy to feel shocked by God's reaction while forgetting about their extreme disobedience.

Scripture teaches that everyone has sinned and falls short of God's glory. The entire earth is guilty. None of us can stand against his perfection and holiness. This is why we desperately need Jesus. He is our victory against sin and death. He is the reason we can stand before a holy God without facing his wrath. Jesus is our righteousness, and he has made a way for us to be with the Father.

Lord, sometimes I struggle to understand the weight of my sin. Give me a deeper understanding of your holiness and undeserved mercy.

Scripture Reading: Isaiah 25-28

Restoring Justice

In that day the LORD of hosts will be a crown of glory,
and a diadem of beauty, to the remnant of his people,
and a spirit of justice to him who sits in judgment,
and strength to those who turn back the battle at the gate.

ISAIAH 28:5-6 ESV

God's restoration of all things includes the restoration of true justice. God is the author of all that is good, right, and fair. He is the only capable judge because he sees into the hearts of man. He knows the nuances of every situation, and he has the perfect solution for every problem we face. He promises to make all things right when his kingdom is fully established on the earth.

We can look forward to that day with great anticipation. There is so much about life on earth that is unfair. There is so much suffering that we cannot understand, and we often see wickedness prosper. It's confusing, frustrating, and beyond our ability to fix. This is why we must put our hope in God's kingdom. He will rule and reign perfectly. We can trust that he is wise, good, and always full of mercy.

Lord, I trust you with the restoration of all things. Help me look to you instead of being discouraged and distraught about the world.

Scripture Reading: Isaiah 29-32

More than Words

"Because this people approaches Me with their words
And honors Me with their lips,
But their heart is far away from Me,
And their reverence for Me consists of the commandment of men that is taught."

Isaiah 29:13 NASB

Jesus quoted today's verse during one of his dramatic confrontations with the Pharisees and the teachers of the law. He claimed that they said all the right things but only pretended to be faithful to God. Jesus then explained that man's righteousness would be uprooted, but anything planted by the Father would remain.

The passage Jesus quotes from Isaiah 29 describes how the so-called wise men of Israel would be conquered and would perish because of their false teaching. God doesn't want us to honor him with our mouths while remaining far from him in our hearts. He wants our whole-hearted devotion. He longs for us to give him everything we have so that we can experience the freedom found in an unhindered relationship with him.

God, may my desire of my heart and the words of my mouth be aligned with you completely.

Scripture Reading: Isaiah 33-36

Good News

With this news, strengthen those who have tired hands, and encourage those who have weak knees.

Isaiah 35:3 NLT

Half-way through his book Isaiah's prophecies turn toward a more consistent theme of restoration. His message of judgment had been declared, and a time of darkness was foretold. He goes on to describe how God will make everything right again. He wants to reassure the people that hope is not lost.

God does not leave us to suffer under the devastation of our sin. He is a God who reconciles and redeems. Part of that process is understanding our desperate need for him, but he always comes through. He faithfully mends what is broken and restores what is lost. He offers us freedom and mercy despite our unfaithfulness.

Lord, thank you for fulfilling your promise of redemption through Jesus. Thank you for the hope I have in his resurrection.

Scripture Reading: Isaiah 37-40

Good Shepherd

He tends his flock like a shepherd:
He gathers the lambs in his arms
and carries them close to his heart;
he gently leads those that have young.
ISAIAH 40:11 NIV

In this chapter Isaiah reminds us that there is no one like God. He doesn't need anyone's help, and he doesn't need anyone's advice. He can't be compared to any gods before him or any we might come up with now. He is the everlasting God and the Creator of the earth. He does not grow weary, and he has everything we need.

God offers us practical help and spiritual guidance. He sustains us, and he is the Shepherd of our hearts. He fills our lungs with breath and comforts us when we need it. He tenderly watches over us and shelters us from harm. He doesn't simply demand we worship him; he gathers us in his arms and holds us closely. He is mindful of our weaknesses, and he helps us overcome them.

God, thank you for the promises of hope in this chapter. You are my Good Shepherd, and I look to you for strength today.

Scripture Reading: Isaiah 41-44

Find Encouragement

"I am he who blots out your transgressions for my own sake, and I will not remember your sins."
ISAIAH 43:25 ESV

The Lord showers his people with intimate messages of assurance. His joy and love overflow through the pages of Scripture. If we are willing to look, we will find redemption for the past, help for our present troubles, and hope for the future. We are blessed to have unlimited access to the Word of God.

There are certain aspects of our faith that we can begin to take for granted. Scripture is filled with simple and miraculous truths. If we dwell on them instead of glazing over them, our hearts will be softened toward their impact. Truth and encouragement are often less complicated than we make them. Everything we need can be found in the pages we are blessed to have in front of us.

Lord, thank you for simple and impactful truth. May your Word permeate my heart and have a profound impact on my life.

Scripture Reading: Isaiah 45-48

Turn to God

"Turn to me and be saved,
all you ends of the earth;
for I am God, and there is no other."
ISAIAH 45:22 NIV

In the middle of Isaiah, the Lord appeals for people to turn to him and be saved. He mercifully offers them a chance to change their ways. He urges them to repent and follow him instead of their own sinful desires. He knows where both paths lead, and he longs for his people to stay close to him.

We know that judgment is coming. We also know that God wants to rescue each of us. All it takes is turning toward him. That is the message of good news proclaimed throughout the book of Isaiah. It is a hard message, but it is also the most encouraging message that could ever be shared. Sin and rebellion have brought death and destruction, but the Lord has provided a way for rescue!

God, thank you for the assurance of your salvation. Thank you for giving me freedom from my sin.

Scripture Reading: Isaiah 49-52

Light of God

Who among you fears the LORD
and obeys his servant?
If you are walking in darkness,
without a ray of light,
trust in the LORD
and rely on your God.

ISAIAH 50:10 NLT

Our perception is limited, and our weaknesses are many. We might have days or even seasons of life when we think we have it all figured out, but that feeling is fleeting and unreliable. The truth is that we are in desperate need of a Savior. He offers us freedom and eternal life that we cannot muster up for ourselves. His light and warmth will never fade.

Our Savior is Jesus Christ. He is the one who set his face like a stone and did what was required to loosen our chains and liberate us from death. Jesus accomplished the Lord's will and did what no one else could do. His work on the cross provided us with salvation. He is more than worthy of our devotion and obedience. His light shines in the darkness forever, and we have the privilege of trusting him.

Lord, forgive me for trying to live in my own light. Help me lean on you and rely on your strength.

Scripture Reading: Isaiah 53-56

Suffering Servant

He was pierced because of our rebellion,
crushed because of our iniquities;
punishment for our peace was on him,
and we are healed by his wounds.

Isaiah 53:5 CSB

The book of Isaiah was written seven-hundred years before Jesus was born, yet every line seems like an eye-witness account of the work and person of Christ. His death is depicted in incredible detail, and his victory over sin is prophesied. His life was clearly prophesied in Scripture, yet he was still rejected by the religious scholars of the time.

Few people expected their Messiah to be a suffering servant. They wanted him to be mighty, victorious, and grandiose. They wanted a king they could brag about. They wanted someone who would valiantly rescue them in a flourish of power. Instead, we have a Savior who was pierced, crushed, and punished. We have a suffering servant who laid down his life for us.

Jesus, thank you for taking my sins upon your shoulders. Thank you for embracing suffering that I might live.

Scripture Reading: Isaiah 57-60

Authentic Religion

"Is not this the fast that I choose:
to loose the bonds of wickedness,
to undo the straps of the yoke,
to let the oppressed go free,
and to break every yoke?"

Isaiah 58:6 ESV

God is frustrated with those who go through religious motions but fail to do the simple things that God expects his people to do. Such people look beautiful on the outside, but on the inside they are full of hypocrisy and wickedness. He constantly reminds his followers that outward actions don't matter as much as heart attitudes.

God doesn't want showmanship; he wants authenticity. He doesn't care how well we perform, and he isn't worried about how productive we are. He never places religion over relationship, and he calls us to the same. Scripture constantly reminds us that his heart is for the oppressed, imprisoned, and hurting. He wants his followers to be more concerned with loving people than with living according to a particular set of rules.

God, help me be genuine in my faith today by seeing the needs of others and doing something about it.

Scripture Reading: Isaiah 61-63

Prepare the Way

Pass through, pass through the gates!
Prepare the way for the people.
Build up, build up the highway!
Remove the stones.
Raise a banner for the nations.

Isaiah 62:10 NIV

The book of Isaiah is a declaration of the Lord's message for the nations. It is the most important news that could be shared. It is a lifesaving, world-changing message. The Savior is coming, and the people must prepare the way! The Messiah is coming, and he will make all the wrong things right!

As followers of Jesus, we each carry this message with us wherever we go. We have the responsibility to share this truth whenever we can. We don't accomplish this through the literal ways listed in today's Scripture. We don't make banners, pave roads, or build structures in preparation for Jesus. Instead, we love each other as Christ loves us. We lay our lives down in response to Jesus' sacrifice so that others might know him.

Lord, may my actions be a good representation of your love. Help me love people in a way that draws them to you.

Scripture Reading: Isaiah 64-66

Ready

"I was ready to respond, but no one asked for help.
I was ready to be found, but no one was looking for me.
I said, 'Here I am, here I am!'
to a nation that did not call on my name."

ISAIAH 65:1 NLT

As the book of Isaiah ends, the Lord pleads one more time for people to call on him. He wants to redeem them, and he wants to save them. He is preparing the world for the coming Messiah who will take the burden of sin upon himself and defeat the grave. He promises to restore his throne to prominence upon the earth. He promises to remove sickness and evil. He is at work even now accomplishing all these things so that people will be saved!

Sadly, many people fail to respond to God's call. They have shut their eyes and closed their ears to the Lord. They have chosen to follow their own ways instead of acknowledging him. Let's turn to the one who is worthy of our attention. Let's heed his call and repent from our sins. Let's offer him our lives and allow him to transform our hearts.

Lord, thank you for being here and being ready to receive me. I am ready to respond to you today! I look to you and I call upon your name! Amen.

Scripture Reading: Jeremiah 1-4

Sent by God

"Do not say, 'I am a youth,'
Because everywhere I send you, you shall go,
And all that I command you, you shall speak.
Do not be afraid of them,
For I am with you to save you," declares the LORD.
JEREMIAH 1:7-8 NASB

When Jeremiah was alive, it was a terrible time to be a prophet. Judah as being threatened by the surrounding nations, and the kings were waffling in their faith. They occasionally showed signs of repentance yet continued to flirt with other gods. In 587 BCE the temple was destroyed in Jerusalem, and the last vestiges of people were taken into captivity. Jeremiah has become known as the "weeping prophet" due to his constant lament for Jerusalem.

Despite the dismal conditions and his personal weakness, Jeremiah was confident that the Lord empowered him to do incredible things. Jeremiah's story is a testimony of what God can do through a willing servant. Jeremiah stood up for God in a culture that was turning away. He confronted powerful rulers and spoke faithfully in the face of opposition.

Lord, though I feel too weak, empower me by your Spirit to serve you. Give me courage to speak the truth and stand strong.

Scripture Reading: Jeremiah 5-8

Easy Burden

"I will go to the leaders and speak to them;
surely they know the way of the LORD,
the requirements of their God."
JEREMIAH 5:5 NIV

Jeremiah expected that the rulers of Judah would respond to the word of the Lord. He expected them to realize that they were on the wrong side of God and that they should repent. He assumed they would be wise enough to listen to God's invitation to return to him. He thought they would be moved by God's warning of destruction if they didn't repent. To Jeremiah's astonishment, the leaders simply refused to respond to God.

Some people think that God's call for repentance is heavy and burdensome. They view him as a dictator who demands obedience. They see his call for surrender in terms of a battle with winners and losers. Jesus teaches that this is the wrong conclusion to make. God's call for obedience is easy and light. He draws us toward himself because he is kind and knows what's best for us. He urges us to surrender because he longs to take care of us not because he is power hungry.

God, I can't continue to carry my own burdens. I surrender to you.

Scripture Reading: Jeremiah 9-12

Valid Frustration

LORD, there is no one like you!
For you are great, and your name is full of power.
JEREMIAH 10:6 NLT

The prophet Jeremiah reprimanded the people for worshipping idols. He called them foolish and stupid. He questioned their intelligence as they put their trust in man-made objects that couldn't talk or respond to them. He passionately questioned why they would put their faith in something that could fall over when the immovable God of the universe longed to be with them.

Jeremiah's frustration is valid, and some of us probably feel this way today. Why does the world seek temporary pleasures when eternal life is available? Why do people worship the beauty of creation without acknowledging the one who created it? Why do we give our devotion to human displays of authority when God speaks in thunder and roars like rainfall? His glory is far beyond anything we can muster up. He alone is worthy of all we have to offer.

Lord, don't let me put my faith in worthless things. You alone are God!

Scripture Reading: Jeremiah 13-16

Agreeing to Treatment

Give glory to the LORD your God before he brings darkness,
before your feet stumble on the twilight mountains,
and while you look for light he turns it into gloom
and makes it deep darkness.

JEREMIAH 13:16 ESV

Most insurance companies love the idea of preventative care. Addressing a problem before it comes to fruition saves everybody time, energy, and money. We would much rather prepare for a potential issue or catch it early than be surprised by it later. It is wise to see what is coming and do our best to equip ourselves for it. An early diagnosis is far better than a late one.

In Jeremiah we can see that the Lord had given Israel the full diagnosis. They were going to die in their sin, but their condition could be cured if they agreed to start treatment. God's required treatment meant that they would have to change their lifestyle and follow his instructions. If they did that, they would be healed. God laid out the options before them, but they had to make the choice themselves.

Lord, examine my heart and treat my sinful condition. Empower me to live according to the instructions you have given me.

Scripture Reading: Jeremiah 17-20

Uncontained

His message becomes a fire burning in my heart,
shut up in my bones.
I become tired of holding it in,
and I cannot prevail.
JEREMIAH 20:9 CSB

Jeremiah was finding it difficult to serve God. He was being mocked every day. People were laughing at him as he was speaking against the ways they were living. He had become a household joke and was called "The Man Who Lives in Terror." He was constantly a contrarian in his own communities. He lamented that he had even been born for his life had become nothing but sorrow. He was tired of sharing God's truth because he was growing tired of people rejecting him.

Jeremiah stayed devoted to the truth despite his incredible hardship. The Word of God was like a fire burning in his heart. He felt he would burst if he tried to contain God's message within him. In the end, it would hurt him more to suppress God's message than to be rejected by people. He knew that it was better to stand with the Lord than with persecutors.

Lord, may my love for you overwhelm my fear of rejection.

Scripture Reading: Jeremiah 21-24

Just and Right

"Do what is just and right. Rescue from the hand of the oppressor the one who has been robbed. Do no wrong or violence to the foreigner, the fatherless or the widow, and do not shed innocent blood in this place."

JEREMIAH 22:3 NIV

Jeremiah called upon the kings of Israel to do what was right. Their reigns were supposed mirror the kingdom of God. That meant that the kings should rescue people from oppression, defend those who had been wronged, treat foreigners with respect, and care for orphans and widows. God wanted the kings of earth to rule their kingdoms according to his values.

There are certain parallels that can be drawn between God's instructions for the ancient kings and how Jesus' kingdom will work. We can assume that God's values have not changed. When Jesus returns to rule and reign on the earth we can be assured that he will honor God's ways. He will rescue the oppressed, lift up the overlooked, give foreigners a home, and care for orphans and widows. He will rule with perfect justice and unending mercy.

God, I want to serve you in your kingdom. Help me do what is just and right.

Scripture Reading: Jeremiah 25-28

What He Wants

"With my great strength and powerful arm I made the earth and all its people and every animal. I can give these things of mine to anyone I choose."

JEREMIAH 27:5 NLT

If God is the Creator and he has authority over everything, it makes perfect theological sense that he would be able to do whatever he wants with his creation. He knows every intricate detail of the universe, and he knows how it all works together. He knows the ins and outs of his people, and he knows what is best for us.

It might seem counterintuitive, but we experience the most freedom when we are surrendered to him. We experience the most satisfaction when we allow him to direct our lives. Our humble submission to his authority is the least we can offer in response to his greatness. He created the universe in power and might, yet all he longs for is communion with his people. He mercifully provides us with everything we need, and he is worthy of everything we have to offer.

Lord, I acknowledge that I am at your mercy today. Direct my steps and accomplish your will through me.

Scripture Reading: Jeremiah 29-32

Good Neighbor

"This is what the LORD of armies, the God of Israel, says to all the exiles whom I have sent into exile from Jerusalem to Babylon: 'Build houses and live in them; and plant gardens and eat their produce.'"

JEREMIAH 29:4-5 NASB

When God's people were taken into exile, they had to figure out how to live away from home in a foreign land. God used the prophet Jeremiah to give them clear instructions. He told them to become good neighbors. He called them to settle into the land, build houses, plant gardens, and eat the produce that grew. He told them to marry, have children, and work for peace in the cities where they lived.

God's commandment to Israel is echoed by what we read in the New Testament. God asks us to honor him by loving others in seemingly normal and mundane ways. The greatest commandment is that we are to love God with all our heart, soul, and mind. The second greatest command, which Jesus says is equal to the first, is that we are to love our neighbor as ourselves. The two commands work in tandem. Giving our hearts to the Lord leads us to lay our lives down for others. In the same way, serving others draws us closer to God.

Lord, I pray for peace and prosperity for my community.

Scripture Reading: Jeremiah 33-36

Unconfined

"In those days and at that time I will cause a righteous Branch to spring up for David, and he shall execute justice and righteousness in the land."

JEREMIAH 33:15 ESV

Jeremiah had been imprisoned by King Zedekiah for confronting him with God's words. Despite his restriction, Jeremiah continued to prophecy. He warned Zedekiah that God would soon be cleansing Judah of its sins. He also reminded Zedekiah of God's promises about the kingdom of David. He prophesied that the Messiah would spring up even though it seemed like the royal line had been cut off. He would rule and reign even though the circumstances seemed impossible.

God fulfills his promises. God uses us and accomplishes his plans even when we feel stuck in our circumstances. His ability to bring his plans to fruition does not depend on our skills or abilities. Our situation does not hinder God from doing his work. He sees the bigger picture, and he knows exactly where we fit.

Lord, release me to serve you today. Accomplish your plans in my life.

Scripture Reading: Jeremiah 37-40

Courageous Kindness

Then the king commanded Ebed-Melek the Cushite, "Take thirty men from here with you and lift Jeremiah the prophet out of the cistern before he dies."

JEREMIAH 38:10 NIV

Jeremiah's words were stirring up anger. Several leading officials got permission from King Zedekiah to arrest Jeremiah and throw him in the bottom of a cistern. An Ethiopian man named Ebed-Melek intervened. He reasoned with the king to release the starving prophet. The king, waffling in his commitments, agreed to let Jeremiah free.

In return for his kindness to Jeremiah, the Lord blessed Ebed-Melek. When it came time for Jerusalem to be captured, the Lord guaranteed to rescue the Ethiopian and keep him safe. Ebed-Melek didn't follow the popular opinion of the day. He spoke up against rulers and authorities who had more power than he did. He honored the Lord, and God rewarded him.

Lord, give me the courage to stand up for others even when I am afraid. Give me boldness and strength to do what is right.

Scripture Reading: Jeremiah 41-44

Take Ownership

"Pray that the LORD your God will show us what to do and where to go."

JEREMIAH 42:3 NLT

This verse provides a subtle hint about the underlying problem in Judah. It was good that the leaders of Judah asked Jeremiah to pray for them. They even suggested that they were willing to follow whatever the Lord said. The issue comes up in the way they address the Lord. They didn't take ownership over their relationship with him. They affirmed that he was Jeremiah's God, but they did not call him their own.

When Jeremiah returned with a word from the Lord, they reacted in disgust. God required them to humble themselves and follow his commands. He warned that their disobedience would result in death. This wasn't what they wanted to hear, and they reacted in anger. It seems that they only cared about God's instructions if they aligned with their itching ears.

Lord, help me follow your ways even when my preferences are different. Give me grace to be obedient to whatever you ask of me. You are my God, and I trust you.

Scripture Reading: Jeremiah 45-48

Choose a Path

"Do you pursue great things for yourself? Stop pursuing! For I am about to bring disaster on all humanity"—this is the Lord's declaration—"but I will grant you your life like the spoils of war wherever you go."

Jeremiah 45:5 CSB

Baruch, the son of Neriah, was the assistant to Jeremiah, and he has an entire chapter of the Bible devoted to him. He helped Jeremiah deliver the prophecies from the Lord, and he shared the trouble and sorrow that Jeremiah experienced. If he wanted a life of respect, fame, and comfort, he wasn't going to get it in the evil climate of Judah.

God mercifully challenged Baruch. He asked him if he wanted to be great in the eyes of evil people. He reminded him that eternal life and goodness come from God alone. He encouraged him that the desires of his heart could not be fulfilled by people. He gave Baruch a clear picture of what his judgment would look like, and he showed him the path to safety.

God, help me seek your kingdom first. I don't need to make a name for myself. I need your name to be great in my life.

September

"My word the comes from my mouth
will not return to me empty,
but it will accomplish what I please
and will prosper in what I send it to do."

Isaiah 55:11 CSB

Scripture Reading: Jeremiah 49-52

Lost Sheep

"My people have been lost sheep;
their shepherds have led them astray
and caused them to roam on the mountains.
They wandered over mountain and hill
and forgot their own resting place."
JEREMIAH 50:6 NIV

Sheep rely on their shepherd to guide them to safe pastures and clean water. Sheep rely on their shepherd to protect them from danger and to shelter them from storms. Ultimately, the Lord is the Good Shepherd for his people. He leads us with strength and wisdom, and he provides us with everything we need.

Israel rejected the Lord and decided to follow false shepherds. They wandered away over mountains and hills. They forgot their home, and they became lost. Their actions left them unprotected, so they were attacked and devoured. Even so, the Lord called out to them, and he searched for them. He promised to destroy those who led them astray. He promised to gather the remnant that survived and return them to their home.

God, forgive me for listening to the wrong voices and going astray. Help me listen to you calling me and remain with you.

Scripture Reading: Lamentations 1-3

Learn to Lament

"Look, O LORD, for I am in distress;
my stomach churns;
my heart is wrung within me,
because I have been very rebellious."

LAMENTATIONS 1:20 ESV

The writer of the book of Lamentations was broken in spirit. He was overwhelmed with grief for the destruction of Jerusalem and the misery of her people. He was overwhelmed with guilt because he realized that his own sin contributed to those consequences. The Lord had sent warnings for hundreds of years through his prophets, yet Israel ignored his voice and turned their back on him. The writer of Lamentations admits that it was their sin that led them into captivity.

As we read this book, we can learn what it means to mourn and lament. Reading about the author's agony reminds us that there is a season for everything, and we don't need to be ashamed of our suffering. Life will have struggles, and Lamentations offers us the reassurance that God will be present through all of it.

Lord, thank you for loving me despite my mistakes. Remind me to turn to you when I am suffering.

Scripture Reading: Lamentations 4-5

A Sliver of Hope

Restore us, O Lord, and bring us back to you again!
Give us back the joys we once had!
Or have you utterly rejected us?
Are you angry with us still?
Lamentations 5:21-22 NLT

We can experience hope and agony simultaneously. The book of Lamentations shows us that they don't cancel each other out. The writer turns to the Lord with the expectation that he will come through. He knows that the Lord is still in charge of all things even when he is in pain.

The author of Lamentations echoes a lament found in Psalm 88. The writer of that psalm is in agony and has a crushed spirit, yet he cries out to the Lord. While there is great pain and loss, he still depends on God because he knows that God is the one who can rescue him.

God, help me lean on you through every season of the soul. You are my rescuer, and I put my hope in you.

Scripture Reading: Ezekiel 1-4

Our Choice

"I will open your mouth and you shall say to them, 'This is what the Sovereign LORD says.' Whoever will listen let them listen, and whoever will refuse let them refuse; for they are a rebellious people."

EZEKIEL 3:27 NIV

The Lord does not force anyone into submission. We all have free will and are in complete control of our decisions. We get to decide whether we will follow him or not. He doesn't coerce us into allegiance because he loves us. He wants us to choose him of our volition. He wants us to willingly offer him our hearts and lives.

God doesn't need people to love him. He is complete within himself, yet he chooses to love us. He chooses to lay down his life for us. He chooses to cherish us and take care of us. He chooses to celebrate our victories and comfort us when we mourn. He gives us the opportunity for relationship, but he doesn't force himself upon anyone.

Lord, give me grace to choose you each day. Thank you for loving me consistently even when I fall short.

Scripture Reading: Ezekiel 5-8

The Lord Is God

"Then they will know that I am the LORD; I have not said in vain that I would inflict this disaster on them."

EZEKIEL 6:10 NASB

Each person will eventually come face to face with God. In that moment, we are either on his side, or we aren't. Understanding God's title and position should stir up confidence. As we recognize who he is, we can be deeply encouraged because we realize that he is on our side, and his ways are good. We can understand that he has our back and will fulfill his promises.

Knowing that the Lord is God could also be deeply discouraging. If we've misplaced our allegiance, his title and position would be daunting. We might have regrets if we've worshipped other things, devoted our lives to the pursuit of self, or refused to acknowledge him. May we be people who come face to face with him and are found faithful in his presence.

God, lead me according to your ways. Draw me closer to you and help me stay faithful to your Word.

Scripture Reading: Ezekiel 9-12

Our Sanctuary

"This is what the Sovereign LORD says: Although I have scattered you in the countries of the world, I will be a sanctuary to you during your time in exile."

EZEKIEL 11:16 NLT

Ezekiel was thirty years old when God called him to prophecy to the people who had been scattered. His message explained why Israel and Judah had been taken into captivity. It also explained the work of restoration that God was about to do. Ezekiel encouraged the people to stay strong because God would see them through their trials. God would be their sanctuary during their exile.

Ezekiel's encouragement applies to us today. There are times when we might feel like foreigners in a strange land. We live in a culture whose values are often the opposite of our own. We might feel like we don't belong and can't find our place. Ezekiel reassures us that our true home is God's presence. He is our sanctuary no matter where we are. Our sense of belonging comes from him rather than our physical location.

Lord, I long to dwell with you. Thank you for being there for me and giving me a place to belong.

Scripture Reading: Ezekiel 13-16

Losing Focus

"Thus says the LORD God: Repent and turn away from your idols, and turn away your faces from all your abominations."

EZEKIEL 14:6 ESV

Israel had been seized by the temptation of sin long before they were taken into captivity. They had already taken their eyes off the Lord and fixed their gaze upon other things. They had been enticed by fame, beauty, and wealth. They forgot about their devotion to God and wandered down the path of chasing temporary satisfaction.

We can learn from Israel's lack of focus. We can clearly see where their distractions lead them, and we can use their story as an example for our own lives. When we feel ourselves beginning to stray, we can repent and turn back to God. He never turns away someone who calls upon his name. He is always merciful toward the heart that humbly asks for help.

Lord, help me remain faithful. Don't let me fall into temptation. Keep my eyes clear and focused on you.

Scripture Reading: Ezekiel 17-20

Repent and Live

"Rid yourselves of all the offenses you have committed, and get a new heart and a new spirit. Why will you die, people of Israel? For I take no pleasure in the death of anyone, declares the Sovereign LORD. Repent and live!"

EZEKIEL 18:31-32 NIV

God's intention for the exile was to give his people an opportunity to remember the life they had while in relationship with him. He wasn't punishing them for the sake of punishment. He longed for them to heed his call and turn back to him. He wanted them to remember that he was trustworthy, faithful, and always good.

We can hear the Lord pleading with his people in Ezekiel 18. His desire is for all people to be saved, and he doesn't want us to suffer the consequences of our sin. He wants us to live and experience the joy of his presence. He wants us to be free rather than enslaved by fleshly desires that don't serve us anyway.

Lord, may your Spirit continue his good work within my heart. Help me choose to honor you rather than follow fleshly desires.

Scripture Reading: Ezekiel 21-24

Follow the Instructions

"Because you have forgotten me and turned your back on me, this is what the Sovereign LORD says: You must bear the consequences of all your lewdness and prostitution."

EZEKIEL 23:35 NLT

We can't live in a way that is contrary to God's standards and expect him to sit idly by. He has given us pages and pages of instructions, and we show allegiance to him by honoring his Word. We don't need to approach the Word with rigidity or fear of condemnation. It's not just a list of rules we have to follow or else. Instead, we view it as a guidebook for finding freedom. Everything God has advised us to do is in our best interest.

Perhaps the best news of all is that God is faithful even when we fail to follow his instructions. He has given us the incredible gift of the Holy Spirit who teaches, convicts, and helps us. He knows that we won't do it perfectly, and he has made a way for us to always return to him. May we strive to honor him with our actions and keep our hearts soft in times of struggle.

Lord, give me courage to confess my sins quickly. Thank you for showing me how to live. Help me follow you for all my days.

Scripture Reading: Ezekiel 25-28

Reassurance

"When I gather the house of Israel from the peoples where they are scattered, I will demonstrate my holiness through them in the sight of the nations, and they will live in their own land, which I gave to my servant Jacob."

EZEKIEL 28:25 CSB

God made a promise to Abraham, Isaac, and Jacob, and he fulfilled that promise from generation to generation. He led Moses though the Exodus and showed him the Promised Land. He helped Joshua establish the tribes and make their homes. He promised David that one of his descendants would reign from the throne in Jerusalem forever.

God always had his covenant promise in mind, so he reminded Israel that he would gather them from everywhere they'd been scattered and return them to live in the Promised Land. This was his plan, and he guaranteed it would come to fruition. He reassured Israel that he would not let them down even when it looked like the plan wasn't working.

God, your commitment to your plan of salvation gives me hope and courage. I trust you to accomplish your will in my life.

Scripture Reading: Ezekiel 29-32

Trusting God's Plans

"On that day I will cause a horn to spring up for the house of Israel, and I will open your lips among them. Then they will know that I am the LORD."

EZEKIEL 29:21 ESV

Throughout his prophecies, Ezekiel explained that the Lord was using King Nebuchadnezzar as his servant. The King of Babylon was the Lord's chosen instrument of destruction. Through Nebuchadnezzar, the Lord orchestrated the scattering of hundreds of thousands of people. As a result, the seed of the gospel was planted across thousands of miles of territory. Generations of Jewish men and women spread around the world looked forward to the day when the Messiah would come.

About six-hundred years after Nebuchadnezzar, the news about Jesus Christ spread rapidly and took root in communities that knew Ezekiel's prophecies. It may be difficult for us to understand why God allows things to happen sometimes, but we can trust that what he does points people to him. His plans are often beyond our understanding, but he is faithful and good.

Lord, help me trust your plans even when I don't understand. Increase my faith and help me keep my eyes on you.

Scripture Reading: Ezekiel 33-36

He Pursues

"I myself will search for my sheep and look after them. As a shepherd looks after his scattered flock when he is with them, so will I look after my sheep. I will rescue them from all the places where they were scattered on a day of clouds and darkness."

Ezekiel 34:11-12 NIV

God pursues his people. This has been true from the very beginning. He called out to Adam and Even in the garden, and he calls out to us now. He sought after Israel even when they were unfaithful, and he seeks us when we are unfaithful. He does not give up on his people. He has proven his faithfulness up until now, and we can trust that he will continue to be faithful.

God longs for you to be near him. He longs to have a close relationship with his people. He wants to walk with us and lead us through life. He is steady, reliable, and capable of caring for us. He shows up when we call for him, and he waits patiently when we wander. He pursues us and draws us back to his heart. We are blessed to serve a God who never quits!

Lord, you are my shepherd, and I lack nothing. You seek me, find me, and restore me. Thank you for loving me!

Scripture Reading: Ezekiel 37-40

Breath of God

"Speak a prophetic message to the winds, son of man. Speak a prophetic message and say, 'This is what the Sovereign LORD says: Come, O breath, from the four winds! Breathe into these dead bodies so they may live again.'"

EZEKIEL 37:9 NLT

The Hebrew word for breath is *ruach.* We know that the *ruach* of God hovered over the surface of the deep in Genesis. The same word is used later to describe the breath that he breathed into Adam to give him life. Here, in Ezekiel's vision, the same word is used when God breaths life into the dry bones and they come back to life. God told Ezekiel that those bones represented the people of Israel.

The Holy Spirit breathes life into those who are not living. He breathes hope into those who are hurting. He breathes restoration into those who are broken. God has been doing this for all of time. The same power that brought Adam to life and restored dry bones lives in us. When we gave our lives to Jesus, God gave us the incredible gift of his Spirit.

God, thank you for the gift of your Spirit. Thank you for breathing new life into me.

Scripture Reading: Ezekiel 41-44

Long-term Vision

Then he led me to the gate, the gate facing east; and behold, the glory of the God of Israel was coming from the way of the east. And His voice was like the sound of many waters; and the earth shone from His glory.

EZEKIEL 43:1-2 NASB

In his powerful vision, Ezekiel was taken to Jerusalem. A man whose face shone like bronze showed him the gates of the temple, giving him details that included dimensions and decorations. The Spirit of God then took Ezekiel to the inner courtyard of the temple where the Lord's voice spoke to him saying, "I will live here forever among the people of Israel."

When Ezekiel had this vision, the temple of Jerusalem had already been ransacked and destroyed. It would be a couple of generations before any Jewish leaders were allowed back to Jerusalem to rebuild. The prophecy spoke to the physical rebuilding of the temple as well as God's eternal plan to dwell within man through his Holy Spirit.

Lord, I trust you to do accomplish things that will extend beyond my lifetime. Give me the faith to see what you can and will do.

Scripture Reading: Ezekiel 45-48

The Lord Is There

"The circumference of the city shall be 18,000 cubits. And the name of the city from that time on shall be, The LORD Is There."

EZEKIEL 48:35 ESV

The last words of Ezekiel's immense, prophetic book are the Hebrew words *Yahweh Shammah*. These words mean, "The Lord is There." These are remarkably hopeful words for a book that began in the chaos of exile. These words point to the Lord's promise that he would restore his throne in Jerusalem and bring his scattered people home.

Could these words be said of you? Could someone point to your life and say that the Lord is there? Would people see the Lord's righteousness and hope shining from the way you lived? Would people hear the Lord's words on your lips and see his care extended from your hands? Would they know that the Lord had chosen to make his home in your life?

Lord, make your dwelling within me. I pray that others will notice the work of your Spirit in my life.

Scripture Reading: Daniel 1-4

Earning Respect

In every matter of wisdom and understanding about which the king questioned them, he found them ten times better than all the magicians and enchanters in his whole kingdom.

DANIEL 1:20 NIV

Four young men were taken hostage from Judah and exiled to Babylon. They greatly impressed King Nebuchadnezzar. These young men had been selected to join a training program meant to acclimate the best hostages into the kingdom of Babylon. These men would be trained for three years in the languages and customs that would enable them to serve effectively in the royal palace.

The four young men refused to compromise their faith, but their approach was not hostile. While showing tremendous respect, they reasoned with the chief of staff. Their humble yet confident attitude won over the attendants in the palace. It became evident to everyone that these young men had excellent health and extraordinary intelligence. God was with them, and everyone noticed.

Lord, help me win people over through a respectful attitude, trustworthy skills, and effective work. May you be glorified in my life above all else.

Scripture Reading: Daniel 5-8

Courage and Integrity

Then the other administrators and high officers began searching for some fault in the way Daniel was handling government affairs, but they couldn't find anything to criticize or condemn. He was faithful, always responsible, and completely trustworthy.

Daniel 6:4 NLT

The leaders in the palace were against Daniel, but they couldn't find anything wrong with him. He lived with integrity, and his steps were blameless. Much to their disappointment, they could find no fault in him. They realized they would need to resort to manipulation in order to bring Daniel down. So, they crafted a law that they knew Daniel would have to break. It was a law that would force Daniel into a corner. He would have to choose between God and the King.

There are two questions for us to consider here. First, where are the faultless and blameless leaders? We've come to a place where we often expect failure from our church and ministry leaders. Second, if faced with a law that explicitly expects us to reject God, would we follow the law? Perhaps now is a good time to assess where our allegiance lies.

God, let me be a man of courage and integrity like Daniel.

Scripture Reading: Daniel 9-12

The Ongoing Battle

"At that time shall arise Michael, the great prince who has charge of your people. And there shall be a time of trouble, such as never has been since there was a nation till that time. But at that time your people shall be delivered, everyone whose name shall be found written in the book."

DANIEL 12:1 ESV

Daniel's final vision seems aligned with the great revelation of John at the end of the Bible. A battle is coming between righteousness and the powers and principalities of the world. This battle will cause tremendous suffering and destruction. Those who remain faithful to the Lord will find salvation. Those who endure to the end will be saved. They will be rescued from the full destruction to come.

There is a world that we see, but there is also a battle going on in an unseen world. From the first page to the last, the Bible depicts an epic conflict. The devil and his demons have waged war against God and his creation. Mighty angels continue to battle behind the scenes to protect God's people. At the end of all things, the Lord and his heavenly armies will be victorious.

Lord, open my eyes to the battle going on. Give me courage and strength by your Spirit to face what's ahead.

Scripture Reading: Hosea 1-4

Always Faithful

"There is no truth, no faithful love,
and no knowledge of God in the land!"
HOSEA 4:1 CSB

The Prophet Hosea lived a remarkable life. The Lord had told him to fall in love and marry a prostitute named Gomer. When Gomer continued in her prostitution, the Lord asked Hosea to have mercy on her and redeem her at his own expense. This happened so that Hosea would have a visual example of God's relationship with Israel.

The Lord loved Israel and had chosen her to be his bride. Though he was faithful to her, she repeatedly prostituted herself to other gods. The Lord's heart broke for Israel, and he chose to have mercy. He redeemed Israel, and he ultimately redeemed us through Jesus. Hosea is a powerful reminder that God's faithfulness does not depend on our ability to stay faithful.

Lord, I am so sorry for my sin. I am sorry for all the times I've chosen other loves. Keep my heart solely committed to you.

Scripture Reading: Hosea 5-8

Acknowledge God

"I desire mercy, not sacrifice,
and acknowledgment of God rather than burnt offerings."
HOSEA 6:6 NIV

The Lord does not expect us to pay him back. We wouldn't be able to do it anyways. The debt we own is too significant. We can't earn forgiveness or salvation. We can't sacrifice enough animals, fast enough days, or tithe enough money to earn right standing with him. We simply cannot do anything to even the score.

God just wants us to acknowledge him. He wants us to call upon his name and let him do the work. He is happy to pay the price because he knows we cannot rescue ourselves. He generously redeems us and restores us to his presence. All he asks is that we look to him, trust him, and love him wholeheartedly.

Lord, I surrender myself to you. Thank you for paying the penalty for my sin. I acknowledge you as my Lord and Savior today.

Scripture Reading: Hosea 9-11

A Fertile Heart

"Plant the good seeds of righteousness,
and you will harvest a crop of love.
Plow up the hard ground of your hearts,
for now is the time to seek the LORD,
that he may come
and shower righteousness upon you."
HOSEA 10:12 NLT

Here in Hosea, God reminds his people of his simple call. "Plow up the hard ground of your hearts," he cried. "Now is the time to see the Lord," Hosea pleaded. He knew that the Lord wanted to plant his kingdom within them if only they would turn their hearts toward him. For generations God has been asking his people to let him move within their lives.

Jesus would later tell a parable about scattered seed. Some of the seeds fell on rocky soil, some on a hardened path, and some among thorns. Nothing could grow in those hostile environments, but some of the seeds fell into fertile soil and produced grain a hundredfold. In other words, if our hearts are soft toward God, he will bear fruit in our lives. Our job is to remain open to his work, and he does the rest.

Lord, don't let my heart be hardened. Let your kingdom flourish within me.

Scripture Reading: Hosea 12-14

Transgressors Stumble

Whoever is wise, let him understand these things;
whoever is discerning, let him know them;
for the ways of the LORD are right,
and the upright walk in them,
but transgressors stumble in them.

HOSEA 14:9 ESV

So much of the tension of the book of Hosea is in the question of whether the people will listen to the Lord or not. If they listen, they would be healed, and their land would be restored. If they don't listen, they would be handed over to destruction and their land would be taken from them.

Today's verse summarizes the main problem. We are reminded that transgressors stumble in the ways of the Lord. In other words, the reason the people are having a hard time listening is that they are having an easy time sinning. Sin blinds and deafens the heart. It's hard to discern which way the Lord wants us to walk when we can't see or hear him. Sin causes us to maneuver through life in darkness. It causes us to be more concerned with tripping than trusting.

God, I don't want to get caught in a situation where I can no longer see or hear you. Direct my steps today and help me walk in the light.

Scripture Reading: Joel 1-3

Empowered and Equipped

"I will pour out my Spirit on all people.
Your sons and daughters will prophesy,
your old men will dream dreams,
your young men will see visions.
Even on my servants, both men and women,
I will pour out my Spirit in those days."
JOEL 2:28-29 NIV

The Prophet Joel looked forward to the outpouring the Holy Spirit. He would have been thrilled to know that hundreds of years later Peter would quote his words on the day of Pentecost. God faithfully did what he said he would. He poured out his Spirit on all people.

God wants to empower each of us with his Holy Spirit. This has always been a significant part of God's salvation plan. In the days before Jesus, God would fill someone specific with his Spirit. They would accomplish great and mighty works. After Jesus ascended into heaven, God gave the gift of the Spirit to all who call upon his name. He wants to dwell with us and equip us to be witnesses for him throughout the earth.

Lord, empower me with your Holy Spirit to share the gospel of Christ with everyone I meet.

Scripture Reading: Amos 1-3

God Himself

"Do two people walk together
unless they have agreed to meet?"
AMOS 3:3 NASB

The Lord was working with his prophets to warn his people about the impending disaster that would befall Jerusalem. The prophet Amos wanted the people to understand that the prophets of the Lord were speaking the words of God. They were not speaking their own thoughts and opinions. Amos suggested that rejecting the words of the prophets was the same as rejecting God himself.

It is no small claim to declare what God says. His Word is clear, and we can confidently share what we find in Scripture. We should be wary of attributing our own thoughts or opinions to him. We should approach his Word with reverence and respect, recognizing that nothing needs to be added to it. Sharing the truth is a weighty responsibility that we should not take lightly.

God, let me be one of your walking partners. Help me share your Word. Give me a new level of respect and reverence for all you have said.

Scripture Reading: Amos 4-6

Come Back to Me

Now this is what the LORD says to the family of Israel: "Come back to me and live!"

AMOS 5:4 NLT

God wanted his people to respond to the prophecies of Amos. He longed for them to return to him and live. He reminded them of all he had done for them, yet they did not return to him. He urged them to turn away from their idols and pagan rituals, yet they did not return to him. He reminded them of the plagues and terrors he had sent upon them for their wickedness in the past, yet they did not return to him.

God loved Israel so much. He gave them every opportunity to turn from their evil ways and follow him. He was slow to anger then, and he is slow to anger now. As long as we have breath in our lungs, God graciously gives us a multitude of chances to choose him. He calls us to return to him over and over again. He is so incredibly patient. Though his people break his heart, he is long-suffering and merciful.

Lord, give my grace to respond to your voice when you call. Soften my heart and help me follow you.

Scripture Reading: Amos 7-9

The Farmer Prophet

Then Amos answered and said to Amaziah, "I was no prophet, nor a prophet's son, but I was a herdsman and a dresser of sycamore figs."

Amos 7:14 ESV

Amos was not a professional prophet. He hadn't been trained to speak the words of God with eloquence and power. He hadn't gone to seminary to study the Scriptures, and he hadn't apprenticed under another prophet. Amos was a herdsman and a caretaker of fig trees. He was a shepherd and a farmer.

Amos was not trying to make prophecy his career. He was simply being obedient to the call of God. Perhaps we can learn from Amos' approach to ministry. We live in a culture that elevates hustle and wealth above nearly anything else. There is a great temptation to make a profit with everything we do including ministry. What might happen if we simply followed God's voice rather than trying to carve out a career?

Lord, help me minister to your people no matter what my day job is. Teach me how to embrace every opportunity to share your love with others.

Scripture Reading: Obadiah 1

Don't Gloat

"You should not gloat over your brother
in the day of his misfortune,
nor rejoice over the people of Judah
in the day of their destruction,
nor boast so much
in the day of their trouble."

Obadiah 1:12 NIV

For generations, the people of Judah watched the northern kingdom of Israel get ransacked by conquering armies. Previously, the northern kingdom had rejected the Lord and invested in pagan religious practices. Their kings had largely done what was wicked in the eyes of the Lord. As a result, the Lord had sent calamity after calamity upon them.

The kingdom of Judah gloated about Israel's destruction. They smirked because they hadn't been seized, and they hadn't been taken hostage like the Israelites to the north. Eventually, Judah became guilty of the same sins. They turned from the Lord and endured an exile. Their story is a reminder to us to stay humble and refrain from judgment. It's not wise to assume we will never fall.

Lord, keep me from finding pleasure in someone else's judgment. Give me a healthy fear of your commands.

Scripture Reading: Jonah 1-4

Obedient Response

Then the LORD spoke to Jonah a second time: "Get up and go to the great city of Nineveh, and deliver the message I have given you."

JONAH 3:1-2 NLT

When the Lord asks us to serve, we shouldn't resist. His call isn't an inquiry. He's not trying to gauge our interest or test the waters. He wants us to be obedient to his call and trust his instructions. He wants us to do the work he calls us to do because we trust him.

God is a good leader. He is excellent at teaching and guiding his children. He knows all of our weaknesses, and he knows how to help us. He is aware of our shortcomings, and he isn't surprised by our failures. He faithfully leads us along the right path even though we are stubborn, prideful, and sometimes downright foolish.

God, thank you for leading me. Help me respond to your voice with obedience and trust.

Scripture Reading: Micah 1-4

Resolute Faith

Though all the peoples walk
in the name of their own gods,
we will walk in the name of the Lord our God
forever and ever.

Micah 4:5 CSB

Micah was determined to stay true to God even when so many others were giving up on their faith. He envisioned a day when the nations would gather at the Lord's temple and learn from God's teachings. He foresaw a time when the Word of God would go out from Zion and usher in peace. For that reason, Micah refused to give up on God.

It might seem like many people in our society are leaving their faith in God behind. It might seem like many people are giving up on the Lord's teachings and moral standards. There is plenty of chaos and opposition, yet the Lord is still God, and people still need him desperately. We get to decide if we will stay true or walk away. If we hold fast to God's promises, he will lift us up in the end.

Lord, help me stay true to you today. May my resolute faith be an inspiring example for others.

Scripture Reading: Micah 5-7

What Is Good

He has shown you, O mortal, what is good.
And what does the LORD require of you?
To act justly and to love mercy
and to walk humbly with your God.
MICAH 6:8 NIV

The Lord has shown us what is good. At Creation he looked at everything he had made and declared it was good. The world worked in its proper order. There was harmony and peace. There was abundant life and uninhibited relationship. Humanity reflected his image. Adam and Eve walked with God and worked according to his will. It was good.

How can such goodness be restored on this earth? Micah says there are three things required of us in order to make it happen. We are called to act justly, love mercy, and walk humbly with our God. If we ever doubt God's will, we can return to this part of Scripture. Today's Scripture in Micah is God's intention for all of us. The execution will differ, but the heart of the matter remains the same.

Lord, help me honor your instructions in Micah. May everything I do fall under the calling to act justly, love mercy, and walk humbly with you.

October

"If you continue in my word, you really are my disciples. You will know the truth, and the truth will set you free."

John 8:31-32 csb

Scripture Reading: Nahum 1-3

Comfort through Justice

The Lord is good,
a stronghold in the day of trouble;
he knows those who take refuge in him.

Nahum 1:7 ESV

The name Nahum means "comfort." His prophecy against Ninevah was meant to provide comfort to the people of Israel who had been brutalized by the evil Assyrian empire. The Lord promised them justice and refuge after a time of turmoil.

God was mercifully patient with the people of Ninevah. Nahum's prophecy wasn't the first time they were hearing of God's potential judgment. He had already given them a chance to repent through Jonah's warning a century before. As such, Nahum reminds the people that God is slow to anger but great in power. He didn't rush to punish them, and he didn't act hastily. Ninevah willfully turned away from God even though they knew better.

God, when the nations rage out of control, let me place my trust in you to restore justice. Help me stand confidently in your faithfulness today.

Scripture Reading: Habakkuk 1-3

Future Promise

Even though…fields lie empty and barren;
even though the flocks die in the fields,
and the cattle barns are empty,
yet I will rejoice in the Lord!
I will be joyful in the God of my salvation!

Habakkuk 3:17-18 NLT

The third chapter of Habakkuk is the prophet's poetic response to the conversation he had with God in the first two chapters. Habakkuk had complained to God about the unrelenting violence and misery under which people were suffering. He had wondered out loud why God was taking so long to stop the cycle of evil. The Lord responded to both complaints with a future-focused guarantee that all things would be restored to their right order.

God's comfort for our trials doesn't always line up with our preferred timeline. He often reassures us of what is coming and asks us to be faithful. There are definitely times when he offers immediate deliverance, but his faithfulness isn't dictated by whether or not we get what we want. Sometimes he urges us to hold on a little longer.

Lord, give me patience and fortitude as I wait for your promises to be fulfilled.

Scripture Reading: Zephaniah 1-3

Seek the Lord

Seek the LORD,
All you humble of the earth
Who have practiced His ordinances;
Seek righteousness, seek humility.
Perhaps you will remain hidden
On the day of the LORD's anger.

ZEPHANIAH 2:3 NASB

Zephaniah's job was to let the people of Judah know that the Lord's judgment was coming upon them. They had rejected the Lord and served other gods for too long. Zephaniah was warning them that everything they placed their faith in would be wiped out. Their idols, gold, and land would all be destroyed because they had chosen to practice evil rather than follow the goodness of God.

God offered an opportunity for repentance despite Judah's unfaithfulness. He instructed Zephaniah to assure them of God's desire to be compassionate and kind. He is not a God who loves punishment or is eager to see people enslaved by sin. He wants us to experience the goodness of his presence and the glory of redemption.

God, don't let my heart be complacent toward you. Help me take my faith seriously today.

Scripture Reading: Haggai 1-2

Gathering for Work

"This is what I covenanted with you when you came out of Egypt. And my Spirit remains among you. Do not fear."
HAGGAI 2:5 NIV

God's faithful people began to rebuild Jerusalem after the exile. The Lord encouraged them to gather together and get back to work doing his will. He lifts them up and reminds them that he is with them. He reassures them that if they work together in faith, he will bless them. God's words to them were not simply commands, but they were an invitation with a promised reward.

There is something very encouraging about people agreeing to work together to do the Lord's will. The very invitation insinuates that we cannot do it alone. We need the variety of skills we all bring to the table. We need help, encouragement, and accountability from our brothers and sisters. We are all God's people, and he is glorified when we strive for unity.

Lord, don't let me isolate myself or cultivate a private faith. Help me cultivate healthy community.

Scripture Reading: Zechariah 1-4

By His Spirit

"This is what the LORD says to Zerubbabel: It is not by force nor by strength, but by my Spirit, says the LORD of Heaven's Armies."

ZECHARIAH 4:6 NLT

Zerubbabel had undertaken a remarkable task. He was going to rebuild Jerusalem. His work was a central component of God's plan to restore his kingdom. It was a daunting weight of responsibility for Zerubbabel because the city lay in ruins. The walls were shattered, and the infrastructure was destroyed. The temple had been vandalized, ransacked, and demolished.

God called his prophet Zechariah to encourage Zerubbabel in his efforts. God spoke to Zechariah, and he prophesied over Zerubbabel that the work of restoration could only be done by God's Spirit. This is an important reminder that while we use our hands to accomplish a task, it is God's power that makes it possible.

Lord, accomplish your will through me by empowering me with your Spirit.

Scripture Reading: Zechariah 5-8

Mount Zion

"Thus says the Lord: I have returned to Zion and will dwell in the midst of Jerusalem, and Jerusalem shall be called the faithful city, and the mountain of the Lord of hosts, the holy mountain."

Zechariah 8:3 ESV

The book of Zechariah is a clear picture of God's heart. He cares deeply about Mount Zion. It is where he provided a substitutionary sacrifice to save Isaac's life. It is where he established David's royal dynasty. It is where he had Solomon build the temple where he put his Presence. It is where the coming Messiah would enter riding on a donkey's colt. It is where the Savior would provide a way to cleanse people from their sins.

The Lord cares deeply about Mount Zion because it is the central point of God's reign on the earth. His story is perfectly woven together, and his promises are good. From Genesis to Revelation, we can see God's hand at work. He faithfully intervenes on behalf of his people, and he draws us to his heart time and time again. His kingdom is our home, and Zion provides a beautiful picture of our salvation.

Lord, thank you for your plan of redemption. Draw me closer to you and help me honor you with all I do.

Scripture Reading: Zechariah 9-11

The King Is Coming

Rejoice greatly, Daughter Zion!
Shout, Daughter Jerusalem!
See, your king comes to you,
righteous and victorious,
lowly and riding on a donkey,
on a colt, the foal of a donkey.

ZECHARIAH 9:9 NIV

Jesus is all over the pages of Zechariah's prophecy. The Lord promises to send himself to live among his people. He promises that his servant will remove the sin of the people, rebuild the temple, and take his rightful place as priest and king. Zechariah prophecies that the servant king will ride a donkey and save his people like a shepherd saves his flock.

The Old Testament provides a rich and beautiful foreshadowing of Jesus. It's clear that God's plan has always been unfolding. He knew every detail of the story from the very beginning. If we look for glimpses of Christ in the Old Testament, we will be met with a glorious and full picture of redemption. It is so much more than history and genealogies. Each moment of God's story points to Jesus.

Jesus, I praise you! Your plan overwhelms me. I rejoice today in your salvation!

Scripture Reading: Zechariah 12-14

His Name Alone

On that day the LORD will become King over the whole earth—the LORD alone, and his name alone.

ZECHARIAH 14:9 CSB

Zechariah looked forward to a day when God would fully establish his kingdom. He prophesied that those who defied the Lord would be defeated, and those who stood with him would be restored. In his letter to the Philippians, the Apostle Paul speaks of a similar situation. He points to a day when Jesus will be given the name that is above all other names. He declares that all will know who he is, and he will receive the worship he is due.

Those of us who know the Word are without excuse. We know that a day of perfection is coming, and we know that Jesus will be rightfully glorified. We have the privilege of knowing the end of the story. May we offer Jesus our devotion now instead of putting it off. May we give him our lives in preparation for that great day.

Lord, reign in my life. May the desires of my heart and the work of my hands bring praise to your name.

Scripture Reading: Malachi 1-4

Soft Hearts

"My name is honored by people of other nations from morning till night. All around the world they offer sweet incense and pure offerings in honor of my name. For my name is great among the nations," says the LORD of Heaven's Armies.

MALACHI 1:11 NLT

God doesn't need us. That was the harsh message that the prophet Malachi gave to the people in Jerusalem. They wrongfully assumed that God would show gratitude toward them because of their historical and current adherence to religious customs. They thought that their habits and rules would save them even though they acted with complacency toward God.

Entitlement is a dangerous path to follow. It's wrong to assume that God owes us anything. We are the recipients of his mercy and generosity. He is the one who sustains us, and we offer him our lives out of gratitude and devotion. We love him because he loved us first. Maintaining soft, humble hearts will lead to far greater things than selfishly demanding anything from God.

God, forgive me for those times when I have taken you for granted and not given you my best.

Scripture Reading: Matthew 1-4

Immediate Reaction

"Follow Me, and I will make you fishers of people." Immediately they left their nets and followed Him.

MATTHEW 4:19-20 NASB

As Jesus launched his ministry, he immediately invited normal people to partner with him. He walked by the Sea of Galilee and simply spoke to the two men who were fishing. He asked them to follow him, and their response was simple. They left their nets and joined him. Later he came across James and John who were mending a net. He called out their names, and they dropped what they were doing to follow him.

All four of these young men followed Jesus for the rest of their lives. They stopped what they were doing, dropped their own plans, and gave everything they had to him. They trusted him, and they learned from him. They saw an opportunity, and they took it. May we be just as quick to jump at the sound of Jesus' voice.

Lord, don't let me miss the opportunity to follow you today. May I be found faithful and willing to drop everything to follow you.

Scripture Reading: Matthew 5-8

Kingdom First

"Seek first his kingdom and his righteousness, and all these things will be given to you as well."

MATTHEW 6:33 NIV

The way we spend our time, energy, and money reveals our value system. We naturally gravitate toward what is most important to us. If we want to know what our priorities are, we can look at how we make investments. Scripture is clear that if we invest in God's kingdom, everything else will fall into place. If we prioritize God's ways, he will take care of us.

To seek God's kingdom first means that we recognize God's reign over all that we do. In other words, we trust that God has authority and leadership over our lives. We acknowledge that his ways are higher than ours, and we seek to live according to his purposes. We reflect his character with our actions, and we build our lives on the foundation of his sacrificial love.

Lord, I admit there are areas of my life where I do not seek your kingdom or righteousness first. Help me rearrange my priorities wherever needed.

Scripture Reading: Matthew 9-12

Inconvenient Love

"The harvest is great, but the workers are few. So pray to the Lord who is in charge of the harvest; ask him to send more workers into his fields."

MATTHEW 9:37-38 NLT

God's heart beats for the lost and broken. If he pays attention to those who are overlooked, so should we. This isn't always easy or convenient. Those of us with tendencies toward selfishness find it all too easy to make our lives about ourselves. Even those of us who know Jesus and have trusted our lives to him can still turn inward and be self-absorbed. We easily forget that Jesus acted with great care toward us by taking our burdens upon himself.

God wants us to pay attention to the condition of others and do our best to help. He wants us to choose compassion and self-sacrifice over comfort and convenience. He displayed sacrificial love for all to see, and he calls us to lay our lives down in a similar fashion. Deliberately caring for those who cannot offer anything in return is foundational to Christ-like love.

God, help me see people as you see them today. Break my heart for those who need you.

Scripture Reading: Matthew 13-16

The Choice

"If anyone would come after me, let him deny himself and take up his cross and follow me. For whoever would save his life will lose it, but whoever loses his life for my sake will find it."

MATTHEW 16:24-25 ESV

Matthew was faced with a decision when he was asked to follow Jesus. He could not continue living the way he was. It was impossible to remain a tax collector and follow Jesus. In order to follow him, he would have to turn away from his old patterns and tendencies. He chose to lose his old life so that he might find new life through Jesus.

Jesus asks us to let go of certain things as we follow him. He doesn't do this because he is selfish or greedy. He isn't needy, and he doesn't want to steal our fun. The truth is that he knows what is best, and he knows us inside and out. He knows that we cannot serve two masters. We cannot worship him and do exactly what we want. The good news is that sacrificing our lives for Jesus is no sacrifice at all because the reward is so incredibly great.

Lord, keep me from clinging to my old life. I surrender to you. Thank you for giving me everlasting life.

Scripture Reading: Matthew 17-20

With God

"With man this is impossible,
but with God all things are possible."
MATTHEW 19:26 NIV

The rich man wanted to be right with God. He wanted to follow Jesus, but he had a lot of possessions that he didn't want to relinquish. His heart sank when Jesus told him to sell all of his stuff and give the proceeds to the poor. Jesus promised him a rich, heavenly reward, but the man felt stuck. How could he give up the treasures in his hands for something he couldn't see or touch?

Jesus' parable reminds us that most people have a blind spot when it comes to money. Money is an easy example to use when discussing the condition of the human heart because we all interact with it in one way or another. If we can't even overcome our love of money, how can we possibly save our souls by following Jesus? Jesus himself reminds us that we can't save ourselves at all. It's impossible, but with God everything is possible.

Lord, I invite you to chip away at anything I hold onto that doesn't honor you. Help me shape my life in a way that pleases you.

Scripture Reading: Matthew 21-24

Resistance

"This gospel of the kingdom shall be preached in the whole world as a testimony to all the nations, and then the end will come."

MATTHEW 24:14 NASB

Jesus didn't say it would be easy to follow him. In fact, he said the opposite. He told his disciples that there was a good chance they could be arrested, persecuted, and killed for believing in him. They would see many people who would turn away from him and betray him. There would be false teachers and rampant sin that could lead them astray. Despite all of the inevitable backlash, Jesus assured his followers that the gospel would be preached across the whole world.

Resistance to the gospel is expected. If we are following Christ's instructions, we will come up against obstacles of many kinds. The presence of difficulty doesn't necessarily mean we are doing something wrong. It's important to be led by the Holy Spirit, trusting him to keep us on the right path even when we encounter resistance.

Lord, use me to spread the good news of the kingdom and give me strength to endure hardship in your name.

Scripture Reading: Matthew 25-28

As You Go

"Go therefore and make disciples of all nations, baptizing them in the name of the Father and of the Son and of the Holy Spirit, teaching them to observe all that I have commanded you. And behold, I am with you always, to the end of the age."

MATTHEW 28:19-20 ESV

The Great Commission carries an ongoing formula. There is an expectation that the truth about Jesus would be passed from generation to generation. After the first disciples made a second generation of disciples, that next generation would continue the pattern. This blueprint was meant to be followed from the time of Christ until the end of the age. This was no short-sighted plan. This was the plan for all of time.

Making disciples is an overarching call for all believers. It's not specific to those who consider themselves preachers or evangelists. Making disciples is as simple as sharing the truth about Jesus. The way we live, love, and serve the people around us reflects Christ. Fulfilling the Great Commission is as simple as walking with people while pointing them to Jesus.

Jesus, as I go about the routines you have set for me, keep this call of discipleship at the forefront of my mind.

Scripture Reading: Mark 1-4

The Beginning

The beginning of the gospel of Jesus Christ,
the Son of God.

Mark 1:1 CSB

Mark starts his punchy Gospel with a simple but profound sentence. Jesus is the Christ, the long-expected Messiah of Israel, and the promised Savior through whom all the world would be blessed. Jesus is also the Son of God who has been present through all eternity and was incarnated as a man. All of this, Mark says, is just the beginning of the gospel.

As we enter the next section of the reading plan, notice how Mark's account has a sense of urgency. It seems like Mark wanted to give as full a depiction of Jesus as possible while emphasizing the miraculous upheaval his story caused the world. As we read the book of Mark, notice how he constantly encourages his readers to keep up the pace because Jesus Christ, the Son of God, was on the move.

Lord, thank you for giving us your Word and revealing to us what Jesus has done. Stir my heart to share the good news.

Scripture Reading: Mark 5-8

Take Courage

They were all terrified when they saw him. But Jesus spoke to them at once. "Don't be afraid," he said. "Take courage! I am here!"

MARK 6:50 NLT

When God first walked with humanity, it turned into a sad game of hide-and-seek. A storm was brewing in the lives of Adam and Eve because they had disobeyed God and broken their relationship. When they heard the sound of the Lord God walking out to them, they hid in fear. Ever since, all of creation has been groaning for the restoration of an uninterrupted walk with God.

Later, while the disciples struggled through another type of storm on the Sea of Galilee, Jesus came walking out to them. The disciples responded with fear and terror when they saw him walking on the water. Jesus called to them and told them to have courage because he was with them. His desire is that we would experience the peace and safety found in his presence. From Genesis until the end of Revelation, God longs to be near his people and walk with us.

Lord, thank you for walking through life with me. May every step I take be with you by my side.

Scripture Reading: Mark 9-12

First and Last

They came to Capernaum. And when he was in the house he asked them, "What were you discussing on the way?" But they kept silent, for on the way they had argued with one another about who was the greatest.

MARK 9:33-34 ESV

The disciples were a bit embarrassed. They knew they were immature. They didn't want to admit to Jesus that they had just been debating which one of them was the greatest. It was such a petty argument. They knew immediately how foolish it had been to entertain such meaningless discussion. After all, they knew deep down that Jesus was already the greatest.

Jesus knew what they had been arguing about, but he encouraged them rather than reprimanding them. He kindly reminded them that the one who serves others will be lifted up in the end. He explained that true success is only guaranteed by putting others first.

Jesus, don't let me think of myself more highly than I should. Instead, help me be ready to put others first.

Scripture Reading: Mark 13-16

Give Me Courage

Immediately the rooster crowed the second time. Then Peter remembered the word Jesus had spoken to him: "Before the rooster crows twice you will disown me three times." And he broke down and wept.

MARK 14:72 NIV

Peter was passionate about Jesus. He was often the first to jump up to serve or speak boldly on his behalf. Despite his zeal, Peter couldn't figure out what Jesus was up to. It seemed like everything they had been working toward was falling apart. Jesus had been arrested and was put on trial. He had been beaten senselessly, sentenced to death, and was going to be executed on a cross.

Peter cautiously tried to watch what was happening to his Lord. He wanted to stay close to Jesus, but people recognized him. Alarmed by their accusations, Peter denied having any association with Jesus. His intentions were probably good, but Peter didn't persevere when pressed. His testimony is a reminder that none of us know how we will react under intense pressure. Jesus' mercy toward Peter's denial is a reminder that God's love is steady despite our flaws.

Lord, I know I'm as fragile as Peter, and I'm probably not as bold as he was. Please give me courage to stand strong in the face of opposition.

Scripture Reading: Luke 1-4

Good News

"The Spirit of the LORD is upon me,
for he has anointed me to bring Good News to the poor.
He has sent me to proclaim that captives will be released,
that the blind will see,
that the oppressed will be set free,
and that the time of the LORD's favor has come."

LUKE 4:18-19 NLT

When Jesus claimed that this prophecy was about him, he was reading the scroll of Isaiah. These words can be found in Isaiah 61. They were written over 700 years before Jesus read them out loud in the synagogue. They depicted the ministry that the Messiah would have. They are the epitome of the good news we cling to today.

Today's verse is so relevant to the condition of the world. How many of us are poor, captive, blind, or oppressed? We all know someone who needs Jesus today. We ourselves are continuously desperate for him to intervene in our lives. Thankfully, he is the answer to our hearts cry, and he generously provides us with everything we need.

Lord, help me share the gospel with whoever I meet today. Show me opportunities to share your love.

Scripture Reading: Luke 5-8

Strong Foundation

"Why do you call Me, 'Lord, Lord,'
and do not do what I say?"
LUKE 6:46 NASB

If we call Jesus our Lord, our lives should reflect who he is. The foundation of our life must be his love, character, and purposes. Jesus says that building our lives on anything else is like building a house on sand. We are unsteady and unanchored apart from him. Jesus is the reason we can withstand storms and floodwaters.

Jesus is our solid rock. He is the foundation that cannot be shaken. He provides us with stability that cannot be found anywhere else. It doesn't matter how well we plan or how skilled we are at building. Surrendering to him and living according to his ways is the only avenue to freedom, true satisfaction, and eternal life.

Lord, may my life reflect your purposes. Show me areas where I have built on sand and help me reshape anything that doesn't honor you.

Scripture Reading: Luke 9-12

Who I Am

"But what about you?" he asked. "Who do you say I am?"
Peter answered, "God's Messiah."

LUKE 9:20 NIV

Jesus asked Peter who he thought he was. He didn't mince words or waffle around. He was direct and deliberate. We can imagine that Peter might have felt put on the spot. He might have felt unsure or insecure. After all, it might have been intimidated to be quizzed by the Son of God himself.

Scripture says that Peter didn't hesitate. He didn't worry about what anyone else might think, and he didn't shrink back in the face of Jesus' question. He said what he knew was true. He declared Jesus to be the Messiah sent from God. He was convinced of who Jesus was, and he wasn't afraid to proclaim it. May we all have as much confidence as Peter.

Jesus, I pray that I will always be ready to answer this question. You are my Savior and the Lord of my life.

Scripture Reading: Luke 13-16

Welcomed Home

"'We had to celebrate this happy day. For your brother was dead and has come back to life! He was lost, but now he is found!'"

Luke 15:32 NLT

God is in the business of rescuing people. He is constantly searching for those who have gone astray. He longs for them to return home. He has prepared a place for them, and he is ready to celebrate the joyous reunion. He scans the horizon looking for the lost. He calls out their name, and he extends overwhelming grace. He pours out forgiveness, and he stretches his arms out wide.

As followers of Jesus, we are each counted as those who have come home. Jesus celebrates our devotion to him. It doesn't matter if we've followed him all our lives or have recently found faith. He is delighted by each of his children who choose to embrace him. He is so happy when we turn our hearts toward him. He welcomes each of us into his presence without hesitation.

Lord, thank you for being such a kind and welcoming Father! Thank you for loving me and calling me home.

Scripture Reading: Luke 17-20

Inviting Himself In

"Today salvation has come to this house, since he also is a son of Abraham. For the Son of Man came to seek and to save the lost."

Luke 19:9-10 ESV

Zacchaeus hadn't woken up that day expecting to have Jesus in his house. He probably hadn't cleaned all the floors or gathered enough food. He probably hadn't arranged for servants or family to get everything prepared. Jesus had simply and unexpectedly invited himself over as a guest.

Zacchaeus agreed and scurried to get enough food ready for the entourage. He may have run around picking things up and dusting off surfaces. He may have felt overwhelmed by presence of the Messiah in his home, but he would quickly realize that Jesus doesn't care about outward displays of perfection. Even while religious leaders scoffed outside, Jesus focused on Zacchaeus' heart. He just wanted to just be with Zacchaeus and know him as a friend.

Jesus, be a guest in my life today. Invite yourself in and be my friend. May I care more about my relationship with you than the outward appearance of my life.

Scripture Reading: Luke 21-24

Forgive Them

When they came to the place called the Skull, they crucified him there, along with the criminals—one on his right, the other on his left. Jesus said, "Father, forgive them, for they do not know what they are doing." And they divided up his clothes by casting lots.

LUKE 23:33-34 NIV

Jesus considered others ahead of himself even as nails were driven into his hands and feet. He cared for people lost in sin even as two criminals flanked him on the cross. He had pity on people who didn't understand what was going on even as soldiers ridiculed him and gambled over his clothing. He thought about the purposes of his Father even in the midst of incredible suffering.

"Forgive them, Father," he cried out between breaths. These words were the reason he had walked the earth in the first place. These words were a summary of God's great plan for salvation. Jesus came to show us the way to the Father, and he remained faithful to that call until his last breath.

Jesus, what can I say in response to what you have done for me? I am forgiven because you gave up your life. Thank you, Jesus!

Scripture Reading: John 1-4

Deep Questions

"I tell you the truth, unless you are born again, you cannot see the Kingdom of God."

John 3:3 NLT

Nicodemus snuck away to talk to Jesus. He had questions burning on his heart. He knew that Jesus was the one to talk to. Before he could get his question out, Jesus cut in and answered a deeper question that Nicodemus hadn't been aware he needed to ask. Jesus told him, "Nicodemus, unless you are born again, you cannot see the Kingdom of God."

With that, the conversation Nicodemus had intended to have drowned a sea of soul-swirling questions. He couldn't wrap his mind around what Jesus said. Being born again seemed impossible. Jesus assured him he was there to provide eternal life. He himself was the way for Nicodemus to know God. Jesus provides the answers to every question our souls could ever ask.

Lord, thank you for the gift of eternal life. Take my questions and turn my eyes toward you.

Scripture Reading: John 5-8

Clarity of Conviction

Simon Peter answered, "Lord, to whom will we go? You have the words of eternal life. We have come to believe and know that you are the Holy One of God."

John 6:68 CSB

In the book of John, we read that many of the people who had been following Jesus rejected him and walked away. At that, Jesus turned to his disciples and asked them if they wanted to leave as well. Peter didn't hesitate to answer. He replied by essentially asking what their other options were. They knew the truth about Jesus, and they couldn't be convinced otherwise.

There was no way Peter was going to walk away from Jesus. He had come to stake his life on the truth that Jesus was the Messiah. Peter fully trusted that salvation came through the work of Jesus Christ. May we also be so convinced of the gospel that we can't comprehend any other path. May we be so trusting of Jesus and his Word that there is no where else for us to go.

Lord, fill my heart with deep conviction. Strengthen my commitment to you and give me grace to choose you through every circumstance.

Scripture Reading: John 9-12

The Good Shepherd

"I am the good shepherd; I know my sheep and my sheep know me—just as the Father knows me and I know the Father—and I lay down my life for the sheep."

JOHN 10:14-15 NIV

We are meant to follow Jesus as sheep follow a shepherd. We must get to know his voice and learn to trust him. We can do this be reading the Word and learning about his life and character. The better we know him, the more we will recognize his voice. As we develop confidence in his proven faithfulness, we won't be as tempted to follow other voices.

The more we follow Jesus the more we will experience his loving care. He knows exactly what we need, and he isn't stingy or selfish. He longs to protect us, provide for us, and lead us through life. He faithfully leads us to the Father, and he takes care of us every step of the way.

O Lord, thank you for knowing me so well. Thank you for watching out for me today.

Scripture Reading: John 13-15

Authority and Influence

He got up from the table, took off his robe, wrapped a towel around his waist, and poured water into a basin. Then he began to wash the disciples' feet, drying them with the towel he had around him.

JOHN 13:4-5 NLT

Jesus is our meek and humble King. He contained all the power of God within him, yet he chose to lay his life down. He had more authority and influence than most of us will ever have, yet he chose to serve the people around him. He didn't serve in a way that was easy or convenient. He embraced a dirty and seemingly humiliating task with grace and confidence.

Power reveals what's inside the heart of a man. The way we behave when we have authority and influence shows what we truly believe about ourselves and other people. If we prioritize self-preservation or comfort, it's clear that we think too highly of ourselves. If we expect other people to serve us or pay their dues, it's clear we lack humility. Let us embrace the way of the servant King and lift up others with our words and actions.

Jesus, your humility overwhelms me. I am not worthy to be your servant, and yet you are willing to serve me. I praise you, my Savior.

Scripture Reading: John 16-18

Holy Spirit

"When He, the Spirit of truth, comes, He will guide you into all the truth; for He will not speak on His own, but whatever He hears, He will speak; and He will disclose to you what is to come."

John 16:13 NASB

Before he was arrested and crucified, Jesus had a long discussion with his disciples. An important part of what he shared with them involved the Holy Spirit. Jesus said he was going to send the Spirit to them so that would be empowered to spread his message. The Spirit would be their advocate and counselor who would support them in their evangelistic work. The Spirit would convict people of their sin and guide them toward truth.

This same Holy Spirit that Jesus sent to the first disciples is available to us. He is our counselor and advocate. He is our encourager and comforter. He is our compass and our source of wisdom. He reminds us that Jesus is our Savior and God is faithful. He brings truth to mind, and he offers us the power of God in our everyday lives.

Holy Spirit, fill me today. Direct my steps and words so that I might glorify the Father.

November

The LORD gives wisdom;
from his mouth come knowledge
and understanding.

PROVERBS 2:6 CSB

Scripture Reading: John 19-21

Breath of God

"Peace be with you! As the Father has sent me, I am sending you." And with that he breathed on them and said, "Receive the Holy Spirit."

JOHN 20:21-22 NIV

After Jesus was crucified, the disciples gathered in a room with the doors locked. They huddled in fear as the events of his crucifixion were still raw. They were worried that they'd be next in line to be accused and executed by the religious leaders. That's when Jesus chose to make an appearance. He met them in their fear.

Jesus commissioned the disciples and gave them some final instructions. He breathed on them and told them to receive the Holy Spirit. He reminded them of their calling, and he encouraged them to remain faithful to the Lord. He appeared to them in the midst of their fear, and he called them out of it. Jesus breathes new life into his followers just as God breathed life into Adam.

Lord, breathe on me. Let me be a witness for you and help me share the life-giving power of your Spirit to others.

Scripture Reading: Acts 1-3

Poured Out

"You will receive power when the Holy Spirit has come upon you, and you will be my witnesses in Jerusalem and in all Judea and Samaria, and to the end of the earth."
ACTS 1:8 ESV

God knew that the disciples would receive the Holy Spirit and share Christ's message with the world. It wasn't a surprise or a fluke. It had been prophesied long ago in the book of Joel. Joel declared that God would pour out his Spirit on all flesh and that the truth would be known by all. He prophesied that anyone who called upon the Lord would be saved.

The circumstances in Acts are a fulfillment of that prophecy. The time had come, and Joel's words were verified. Jesus' followers gathered in prayer, and men and women of all ages received the miraculous gift of the Holy Spirit. God gave his people exactly what they needed to share his love across the world.

Lord, fill me with your Spirit so that I can be your witness today.

Scripture Reading: Acts 4-6

Fully Confident

"As for us, we cannot help speaking about what we have seen and heard."

Acts 4:20 NIV

Peter and John were arrested by the same people who arrested Jesus. They had every reason to fear the same outcome at the hands of an anxiety-ridden group of religious leaders. The leaders commanded them not to speak or teach in the name of Jesus. The disciples had just seen Christ crucified, so those warnings must have held some serious weight.

Despite the very real threat, Peter and John weren't swayed. They confidently explained that they didn't have a choice but to proclaim what they had seen. They couldn't deny Christ because they were convinced he was the Messiah. They couldn't stay silent because they knew they held the key to eternal life. Their fear might have been real, but their confidence was stronger than their fear.

Jesus, help me hear what you are saying and see what you are doing. Give me confidence to share your love and truth with everyone I meet.

Scripture Reading: Acts 7-9

Expected Suffering

"Go, for Saul is my chosen instrument to take my message to the Gentiles and to kings, as well as to the people of Israel. And I will show him how much he must suffer for my name's sake."

ACTS 9:15-16 NLT

Following Jesus doesn't translate into a cushy life. As nice as it sounds, believing in Jesus doesn't mean an absence of struggles, frustrations, fear, or pain. Jesus clearly told us that we would have trouble in the world. He didn't mince words, and he didn't sugar coat what we were signing up for. He gives all of us the opportunity to count the cost and make a willful decision.

We know the truth, yet we still act surprised when troubles come our way. We have been told to expect difficulty, but we still cry out in desperation when our faith is tested. Following God comes with a certain amount of inevitable resistance, but we are not left alone to flounder our way through it. Jesus also promised us that he himself would be with us through all things. He is present through every trial we face.

Lord, may I lean upon your strength when mine is waning. May I find courage in the truth as you equip me to persevere.

Scripture Reading: Acts 10-12

All People

"He sent the message to the Israelites, proclaiming the good news of peace through Jesus Christ—he is Lord of all."
ACTS 10:36 CSB

Peter knew that Jesus came to earth as the Savior and Messiah. He knew that the religious systems of law and sacrifice would be fulfilled by Jesus. He knew that Jesus was the path to redemption for God's people. He was the fulfillment of every prophecy God had given to Israel. Jesus was the one true King, and Peter didn't doubt it. Even so, there was a bigger picture that Peter had yet to understand.

It wasn't until Peter had a vision from God and an encounter with a Gentile named Cornelius that he understood the wider scope of things. Cornelius helped him see that Jesus was the savior for all people. He offered redemption to Jew and Gentile alike. This meant that God's plan for his people would impact the entire world. His truth wasn't meant to be heard by Israel alone.

God, your salvation is for all people. Thank you for breaking down barriers and calling all of us your children.

Scripture Reading: Acts 13-15

Tell the Story

"My friends, I want you to know that through Jesus the forgiveness of sins is proclaimed to you."

ACTS 13:38 NIV

On Paul's first missionary journey, he was able to present a full sermon in the synagogue on a Sabbath day. After he shared the usual passages, Paul addressed those who had gathered. He walked them through the storyline of Israel's history from the time of captivity in Egypt to the time of the Judges and the kingdom of David. He went on to describe how Jesus' crucifixion and resurrection fulfilled the prophecies about the Messiah.

Paul's oration is a challenge to all of us. We have unlimited access to Scripture, and some of us are well versed in biblical truth. Can we tell the story of salvation from Genesis onward as Paul did? Can we share the history of God's faithfulness alongside the hope of his promised resurrection? May we be people who memorize God's story and store it in our hearts.

Lord, embed the story of your gospel into my mind and heart so that I would be able to share it to others.

Scripture Reading: Acts 16-18

Powerful Partnerships

He found a Jew named Aquila, a native of Pontus having recently come from Italy with his wife Priscilla, because Claudius had commanded all the Jews to leave Rome. He came to them, and because he was of the same trade he stayed with them, and they worked together, for they were tent-makers by trade.

ACTS 18:2-3 NASB

Aquila and his wife Priscilla were among the thousands of Jews who had fled Rome because of the threats issued by the emperor Claudius. Aquila and Priscilla set up a business in the trading port of Corinth making and selling tents. They had already put their faith in Christ before they even met Paul. When he arrived in Corinth, he ended up staying with this couple for quite some time as he was also a tent maker.

While in Corinth, Paul felt empowered to share about Christ even when there was opposition to his message. Many people became believers during this time, and Aquila and Priscilla became trusted partners in ministry. When it came time for Paul to go on to the next stop on his missionary travels, this tent-making couple went with him. Soon, they were raising up other ministry leaders around the Roman Empire.

Lord, surround me with trusted partners in faith and ministry.

Scripture Reading: Acts 19-21

Compelled to Share

"I do not account my life of any value nor as precious to myself, if only I may finish my course and the ministry that I received from the Lord Jesus, to testify to the gospel of the grace of God."

ACTS 20:24 ESV

Paul's primary message was to repent, turn to God, and have faith in Jesus. His message didn't depend on age, background, ethnicity, or social status. He boldly shared the truth with whoever would listen. He devoted his life to sharing God's Word whenever and wherever he could.

We live in a time when there aren't many hindrances to the spreading of news. Nearly the entire world has access to everything right at their fingertips. As such, there seems to be less urgency to spread the gospel than there might have been in Paul's time. He was eager to tell people something they had never heard before. The gospel is still highly relevant despite our culture's oversaturation of information. May we be like Paul and be compelled to share God's Word despite our circumstances.

Lord, stir my heart to share the message of repentance and faith in Jesus. Give me boldness and creativity.

Scripture Reading: Acts 22-24

Unwavering Call

That night the Lord appeared to Paul and said, "Be encouraged, Paul. Just as you have been a witness to me here in Jerusalem, you must preach the Good News in Rome as well."

ACTS 23:11 NLT

Paul caused an uproar among the religious leaders as he described his call to share the gospel of Jesus Christ. After one message he had been bound and whipped by Roman soldiers. After another he was taken under guard to prison for his own safety. That's when the Lord appeared to Paul in Jerusalem and fortified his soul.

For the next few years, Paul remained in prison in Caesarea where he shared the gospel with Roman leaders including King Agrippa of Judea. Eventually, his audience with the King led to the command to transfer Paul's imprisonment to Rome where he could appeal to Caesar himself. Paul never wavered from his call to share the truth.

God, fill me with courage like Paul. Give me boldness to share your message in all circumstances.

Scripture Reading: Acts 25-28

Withstanding Truth

"For this reason I have asked to see you and talk with you. It is because of the hope of Israel that I am bound with this chain."

ACTS 28:20 NIV

Paul began to preach as soon as he arrived in Rome. He wasn't going to waste a moment. The book of Acts ends with him preaching the gospel of Jesus Christ even while under house arrest. We learn that he shared with local Jewish leaders, members of Caesar's household, and Roman soldiers. He proclaimed the kingdom of God even while imprisoned.

Paul's hope couldn't be restrained by shackles and chains. Man made obstacles cannot stand in the way of the truth. There is nothing the world can do to dampen the power of the gospel. God has been faithful to each generation, and his glorious works will be known by everyone. Chrit's light will shine even when the world seems darker than ever. God will still be glorified even when it seems like everything is falling apart.

Lord, thank you for the strength of the gospel. Thank you for truth that withstands no matter what comes up against it.

Scripture Reading: Romans 1-3

Unashamed

I am not ashamed of the gospel, for it is the power of God for salvation to everyone who believes, to the Jew first and also to the Greek.

ROMANS 1:16 ESV

Paul was unashamed of Jesus. He walked upstream during his ministry. Everything he preached was contrary to the popular belief of the day, but he wasn't deterred. He had experienced the transformative power of God, and he wanted everyone to know the truth. He longed for the gospel of Jesus to be shared across the world.

Don't suppress your wonder for God today. Don't be uncomfortable to admit that you know the Creator of the universe. Don't hide the fact that you have a life-changing message embedded in your heart. Don't cower when others threaten to ridicule you for your faith. Boldly rejoice in the truth that has changed your life!

Lord, give me courage to share your love with others. Help me stand strong even when I am opposed.

Scripture Reading: Romans 4-6

Development of Hope

We can rejoice, too, when we run into problems and trials, for we know that they help us develop endurance. And endurance develops strength of character, and character strengthens our confident hope of salvation.

Romans 5:3-4 NLT

We don't do ourselves any favors by cutting corners. While it sounds nice, we can't just skip over suffering and go straight to the reward. As followers of Jesus, our hope isn't tied to our circumstances; it's built by having faith that God will keep his promises. Hope comes from building character which comes from building endurance. Endurance cannot be built by easy circumstances.

We are made stronger by problems and trials. If we choose to depend on the Lord through them, he promises to help us endure. Part of the true Christian life is learning to trust God in the middle of difficult circumstances rather than assuming we deserve a miraculous rescue. Character is the integrity of our conduct and the clarity of our perspective that is grown in the crucible of endurance.

Lord, I don't want an unhealthy or disingenuous faith. Form long-lasting hope in me through every season of my life.

Scripture Reading: Romans 7-9

Unhindered Work

If the Spirit of Him who raised Jesus from the dead dwells in you, He who raised Christ Jesus from the dead will also give life to your mortal bodies through His Spirit who dwells in you.

ROMANS 8:11 NASB

There are not many chapters in the Bible that are more uplifting than the eighth chapter of Romans. It is packed full of powerful verses. We are reminded of our freedom and position in Christ. We are encouraged that nothing can take God's love away from us. We are reassured that the power of Christ is at work in our lives.

The same Spirit that raised Christ from the dead lives in us. We have access to that same power! How many of us live as though we believe that? How many of us wander through our days being subject to our fleeting feelings or unfortunate circumstances? This is not to say that the Holy Spirit's power will magically change our circumstances, but we can be confident that it can change our hearts and attitudes.

God, let the truths of this chapter be deeply rooted in my soul. May your Holy Spirit be unhindered in my life.

Scripture Reading: Romans 10-12

Glorify God

From him and through him and for him are all things.
To him be the glory forever! Amen.
ROMANS 11:36 NIV

The reason we exist is to bring glory to God. He made us, and he sustains us. If we aren't glorifying him with our actions, then it just makes logical sense that things would start coming apart. If we glorify sin, we will have lives that unravel. We might trick ourselves into thinking we are fine, but the truth is that everything will eventually come to the light.

Therefore, don't conform to the patterns of this world. We are all tempted to give glory to things other than God. We all need to be transformed by the renewing of our minds. We don't need to be ashamed of our tendency to stray, but we do need to take responsibility for it. We do need to actively offer ourselves to the Lord and humbly accept his correction. We glorify God when we approach him with confidence, knowing that he is merciful and gracious.

Lord, help me fulfill your purposes for me. May my life bring glory to your name.

Scripture Reading: Romans 13-14

Put On Christ

Put on the Lord Jesus Christ, and make no provision for the flesh to gratify its desires.

ROMANS 13:14 CSB

Throughout the New Testament we are reminded to cast off anything that does not reflect the character of God. We are encouraged to get rid of harmful habits, immoral thinking, and sexual sin. We are called to live above reproach, avoid jealousy, and refrain from quarreling.

Instead, we are called to put on Jesus. As his followers, we clothe ourselves in his character and cover ourselves with his holiness. We wear kindness and gentleness like garments, and we devote our lives to serving others. We choose peace and love over power and personal gain. We don't do these things because we are bound to, but because we trust that God knows what is best. We trust that his standards are fruitful and good.

God, clothe me in your righteousness so that I might display the life-changing hope that only comes from knowing you.

Scripture Reading: Romans 15-16

Glorifying God

May the God of endurance and encouragement grant you to live in such harmony with one another, in accord with Christ Jesus, that together you may with one voice glorify the God and Father of our Lord Jesus Christ.

ROMANS 15:5-6 ESV

Paul reminds us to bear with people who are weak, and this might be one of the most difficult passages of Scripture. We are called to prefer others. This means we must deny ourselves in favor of other people. This doesn't come naturally, and it certainly isn't always convenient. Building up our neighbors, living in harmony with people we don't like, and choosing peace over conflict is difficult but worth it.

If Jesus was thinking about us even while hanging on the Cross, then we should be thinking about the well-being of our family, friends, and neighbors. A self-absorbed, self-serving lifestyle does not reflect the way Jesus patterned his life. We live within a faithful network of believers who seek to serve others in the name of Christ.

Lord, show me opportunities to serve the people around me. Give me grace to be selfless and kind.

Scripture Reading: 1 Corinthians 1-3

Looking Foolish

The message of the cross is foolishness to those who are perishing, but to us who are being saved it is the power of God.

1 Corinthians 1:18 niv

Many people in this world don't understand Jesus. As a result, many people don't understand his followers. The way we live and the choices we make won't always line up with how the world does things. Scripture reminds us that we don't need to be discouraged by those who think the cross is foolish.

What seems like foolishness in the eyes of non-believers is not at all ridiculous to God. The world might see our standards as naïve, old-fashioned, or pointless, but we don't have to worry about what the world thinks. Our allegiance and devotion is to the one true God. We live according to his standards, and we trust that he will keep his promises.

Lord, help me find my value in what you think of me rather than what others think of me.

Scripture Reading: 1 Corinthians 4-6

Personal Temple

Do you not know that your body is a temple of the Holy Spirit within you, whom you have from God? You are not your own, for you were bought with a price. So glorify God in your body.

1 Corinthians 6:19-20 ESV

Scripture has many references to the temple. King David envisioned building a home for God so that he could dwell with his people in Jerusalem. His son, Solomon, built the first temple, and it was a grand structure with a holy place for God's Presence. After the temple was destroyed, it was restored and then rebuilt by Herod just before the ministry of Jesus.

When Jesus made his dwelling among us, he alluded to the destruction of the physical temple. He quoted the Prophets and suggested that God's Spirit would dwell within all those who believed in him. The New Testament writers pick up on this and taught that God's people themselves became a temple within which God would reside through his Holy Spirit.

Lord, live in me today. Help me treat my body as your home. Thank you for dwelling with me.

Scripture Reading: 1 Corinthians 7-9

Set Free

You were bought for a price; do not become slaves of people.

1 Corinthians 7:23 NASB

The expectations others place on us are not the expectations we are supposed to live by. We are not slaves to any other person. We do not have to do something just because someone else tells us to do it. We do not have to be motivated by fear, peer-pressure, temptation, or sin.

We have been set free by the blood of Christ. He paid a ransom for each of us, and he has redeemed us. When we chose to follow him, he released us from the captivity of sin so that we could live in the freedom he created us to have. His standards are the blueprint for our liberty. Our identity is found in his image, and his love is the foundation of our lives.

Lord, thank you for setting me free from sin and death. Help me live a life that honors you.

Scripture Reading: 1 Corinthians 10-12

Only Then

Whether you eat or drink, or whatever you do, do it all for the glory of God.

1 CORINTHIANS 10:31 NLT

Many people live for the weekend. They put up with the bustle of the work week so they can play on Friday and Saturday. They plod through the weekdays so they can eat and drink on the weekends. This can become a frivolous cycle that eventually leaves people empty.

This is reminiscent of what was written in Ecclesiastes. The writer, Solomon, tried to find satisfaction by working then enjoying food and wine. He discovered that without God there was no lasting pleasure in those things. Eating and drinking became meaningless, fleeting pursuits. Every pleasure is a gift from God and was designed to point us back to God. Everything we do is meant to glorify him. Only then will we find freedom and fulfillment.

Lord, I pray that everything I do today will point to you and give you glory.

Scripture Reading: 1 Corinthians 13-16

Dedicated Efforts

My dear brothers and sisters, stand firm. Let nothing move you. Always give yourselves fully to the work of the Lord, because you know that your labor in the Lord is not in vain.

1 Corinthians 15:58 NIV

One of the most interesting trends of our current culture involves the introduction of addictive screen-time activities. Our digital devises have begun to monopolize our time and change the wiring of our brains. We are spending hours doing unproductive things. No generation in history has been more active while accomplishing less. A lot of us are spinning our wheels and getting nowhere.

Paul's words to the early believers in the city of Corinth could redirect us to healthier habits today. He encourages us to give ourselves fully to the work of the Lord. He reminds us that nothing we do for God is in vain. Everything takes on meaning when we focus our lives on glorifying Jesus. Everything has a purpose when we are devoted to pleasing the Lord.

Lord, don't let me waste away the opportunities I have to bring glory to you.

Scripture Reading: 2 Corinthians 1-3

Confidence in Christ

As many as the promises of God are, in Him they are yes; therefore through Him also is our Amen to the glory of God through us.

2 Corinthians 1:20 NASB

Jesus is the yes and amen to all of God's promises. He is the fulfillment of every promise God has made to his people. Jesus is the answer to our searching, longing, and striving. He is the solution to our greatest problem. Mankind is incomplete and lost without God, and Jesus made a way for us to be with God. We were created to be in an unhindered relationship with our Maker, and Jesus bridged the gap we could not cross.

We might think that possessions, titles, or a completed to-do list will satisfy our needs. We might think that satisfaction comes from those things. The truth is that all our needs are met in the presence of God. He is the answer to our soul's deepest longings. He alone can satisfy us. We will find what we are looking for when call upon the name of Jesus and seek the presence of our Father.

Lord, thank you for gift of Jesus. Thank you for making a way for me to be with you. You are all I need.

Scripture Reading: 2 Corinthians 4-6

Clay Jars

We have this treasure in jars of clay, to show that the surpassing power belongs to God and not to us.

2 Corinthians 4:7 esv

Paul taught about having unwavering confidence in the first chapter of his letter to the Corinthians. He reminds us that confidence is not the result of human wisdom or determination. The source of our confidence is Jesus Christ. His trustworthiness and power are the basis our assurance.

After all, we are fragile like jars of clay. We are not made to withstand harsh circumstances on our own. We are easily broken, and we aren't very durable. Our strength comes from God who is far greater than our imperfections. His glory is magnified in our weakness, and the great value of his treasures are seen even more clearly when displayed by our humble lives.

Lord, use me even though I'm a fragile jar of clay. May your strength be magnified by my weaknesses.

Scripture Reading: 2 Corinthians 7-9

Joyful Generosity

God will generously provide all you need. Then you will always have everything you need and plenty left over to share with others.

2 Corinthians 9:8 NLT

The Bible teaches us to be open-handed toward others. We are called to live generously and hold our blessings with open hands. When we are tempted to focus on what is fair or even, we should remember that God is the one who provides for us in the first place. Every good gift comes from his hands, and we are simply called to be good stewards.

We should hold loosely to our possessions while holding tightly to Christ. Joyful generosity reveals the character of Christ. When we trust him to provide for us, we can let go of the anxiety that comes from worrying about our physical circumstances. Instead, we can give that time and energy to loving others and helping meet the inevitable needs we see all around us.

Lord, show me opportunities to be generous. Thank you for the many good gifts you've given me.

Scripture Reading: 2 Corinthians 10-13

Boast in the Lord

Let the one who boasts, boast in the Lord. For it is not the one commending himself who is approved, but the one the Lord commends.

2 Corinthians 10:17-18 CSB

Boasting in the Lord shows an understanding of his sovereignty and power. If we know who he is and what he's done, there really isn't another choice. How can we boast in our success when God has orchestrated our lives? How can we boast in our riches when every good gift comes from his hands? How can we boast in our talents when he is the one who formed us?

What does it look like to boast in God? We can practice giving him the credit rather than taking it for ourselves. We can humbly ask him for help and acknowledge his provision. We can be mindful of our desire for approval, and we can repent when we are too focused on impressing people. We can readily admit our flaws and look for opportunities to grow in love and service.

God, let me call attention to you today and boast in who you are. Help me grow in humility as I worship you.

Scripture Reading: Galatians 1-3

No Longer I

"I have been crucified with Christ and I no longer live, but Christ lives in me. The life I now live in the body, I live by faith in the Son of God, who loved me and gave himself for me."

GALATIANS 2:20 NIV

Surrendering our lives to Jesus is not simply a matter of words or intentions. When we choose to follow him, we give him access to our hearts, and we trust him with the leadership of our lives. We listen to his instructions, and we deliberately follow the path he lays out for us. If we choose to follow the Lord but nothing in our life changes, it might be time for some self-reflection.

Some of us might balk at the idea of surrendering. We don't want to give up control, or we feel defensive about the way we want to live. It's important to understand that Christ living in us and through us is not burdensome. His ways are good, and everything he does is loving. We can trust his leadership even when it's contrary to our preferences because we know that he is our worthy and kind Savior.

Lord, I am realizing how much I need to rely on your Holy Spirit to sanctify my life. Soften my heart and help me follow you.

Scripture Reading: Galatians 4-6

Spirit Led

Since we are living by the Spirit, let us follow the Spirit's leading in every part of our lives.

GALATIANS 5:25 NLT

The Spirit of God is at work in our lives. He lives within us and compels us to pursue Christ. He chips away at those unnecessary and unhelpful things we have added to our souls. He reveals God's goodness to us and gives us a desire to please him with our conduct.

While the sinful nature tempts us to do things that oppose God, the Spirit produces all kinds of good fruit in our lives. The Spirit empowers us to follow Jesus, and Jesus advocates for us before the Father. The Spirit helps us when we need guidance, and Christ offers us his righteousness. Through Christ's sacrifice and the power of the Holy Spirit, we have everything we need to honor God.

God, thank you for helping win the battle that rages inside. Fill my life with good fruit.

Scripture Reading: Ephesians 1-3

God's Power

I also pray that you will understand the incredible greatness of God's power for us who believe him. This is the same mighty power that raised Christ from the dead and seated him in the place of honor at God's right hand in the heavenly realms.

EPHESIANS 1:19-20 NLT

The Apostle Paul wanted the Ephesian Christians to realize that God's Holy Spirit was ready to give them power. His prayer was that they would grow in the wisdom and knowledge of God and have full confidence in him. Ultimately, he wanted them to live by the power of the Spirit through their belief in Jesus. After all, the same power that raised Jesus from the dead was available to them.

We can live by the power of God today. We don't need to seek empowerment or strength from any other source. We have access to the very throne room of God. Jesus died and rose again so we could have unlimited access to God and all he offers us. When we believe in his resurrection and call upon his name, he strengthens us from the inside out.

Heavenly Father, make me strong through the resurrection of Jesus Christ and the power of his Holy Spirit.

Scripture Reading: Ephesians 4-6

As Christ Walked

Walk in love, as Christ loved us and gave himself up for us, a fragrant offering and sacrifice to God.

EPHESIANS 5:2 ESV

We are meant to walk like Jesus walked. Our steps should mimic his steps. If Christ walked in love, we should strive to do the same. If Christ walked through the streets, carrying his cross, we should be willing to carry our own. His entire life was devoted to honoring his Father, and we are called to follow his ways.

Our devotion to Jesus is a fragrant offering to God. He doesn't want us to drum up a sacrifice for him. He doesn't want us to come up with something we think is worthy. All he asks is that we follow his Son, and the Son leads straight to his heart. He asks us to follow Jesus because he knows that's how we will find him.

Lord, keep me from walking on my own path with my own stride. May I walk fully in the love of Christ, offering myself to you and to others today.

Scripture Reading: Philippians 1-4

Your Citizenship

Above all, you must live as citizens of heaven, conducting yourselves in a manner worthy of the Good News about Christ. Then, whether I come and see you again or only hear about you, I will know that you are standing together with one spirit and one purpose, fighting together for the faith, which is the Good News.

PHILIPPIANS 1:27 NLT

As God's children, our citizenship is in heaven. Our days on this earth are merely temporary, and it is not our true home. We are first and foremost members of God's kingdom. Our words and actions should reflect his character and purposes. The way we live should be an obvious clue as to where we are from.

Are you living according to your citizenship today? Do you recognize the authority you live under? Do your commitments and convictions reflect the values of the kingdom to which you belong? Do you rejoice over the things that your king rejoices over? Do you mourn over the things that break his heart? Do you live in such a way that others would know that your citizenship comes from heaven?

God, you are my King, and I want my life to reflect your values. Give me grace to be a positive representative of your kingdom.

December

Whatever was written in the past was written for our instruction, so that we may have hope through endurance and through the encouragement from the Scriptures.

Romans 15:4 CSB

Scripture Reading: Colossians 1-4

Represent Christ

Be wise in the way you act toward outsiders; make the most of every opportunity. Let your conversation be always full of grace, seasoned with salt, so that you may know how to answer everyone.

Colossians 4:5-6 NIV

We are representatives of Jesus. When we chose to follow him, we surrendered our lives and made a commitment to live according to his ways. Our actions reflect upon him. The way we live and interact with others should give the world a glimpse of who Jesus is.

May our words be kind and life giving. May we take every opportunity to serve those around us with joy and generosity. May we remember that our words matter, and even the smallest interaction with someone can make a difference. Remaining soft hearted toward the instruction of the Holy Spirit is how we ensure that our actions reflect Christ's love and character.

Lord, may your love overflow to the people around me. Help me take advantage of every opportunity to honor you.

Scripture Reading: 1 Thessalonians 1-3

Inspired by Others

We recall, in the presence of our God and Father, your work produced by faith, your labor motivated by love, and your endurance inspired by hope in our Lord Jesus Christ.

1 Thessalonians 1:3 CSB

Paul told the believers in Thessalonica that he always gave thanks to God for them. He told them that he prayed for them constantly because they were always on his mind. Their hard work for Christ inspired him greatly.

We are all members of the same body. It's encouraging when other believers are strengthened in their faith, and we can trust that our testimonies offer encouragement right back. A victory for one is a victory for all. Sometimes we will experience personal success, and we can always rejoice at the success of others.

Lord, help me remember that we are all part of the same body. Teach me how to rejoice with the successes of others.

Scripture Reading: 1 Thessalonians 4-5

Live a Quiet Life

Make it your goal to live a quiet life, minding your own business and working with your hands, just as we instructed you before. Then people who are not believers will respect the way you live, and you will not need to depend on others.

1 THESSALONIANS 4:11-12 NLT

People who are not followers of Jesus often struggle with those who claim to be Christians but whose conduct doesn't reflect the way Jesus lived his life. Hypocrisy within the Church causes more damage than we probably realize. It's not a matter of being perfect all the time, but it is a matter of humbly approaching our shortcomings and being mindful of how we live.

Paul encourages the new believers in Thessalonica to live hard-working, trustworthy lives among their neighbors. He urges them to quietly mind their business and stay in their lane. He teaches them to earn the respect of others and to be careful not to become a drain on the community. Over time, their conduct will win people over to the life-changing truthfulness of Jesus Christ.

Jesus, give me fortitude to live with integrity today. Help me live in a way that reflects you.

Scripture Reading: 2 Thessalonians 1-3

Success by Faith

With this in mind, we constantly pray for you, that our God may make you worthy of his calling, and that by his power he may bring to fruition your every desire for goodness and your every deed prompted by faith.

2 THESSALONIANS 1:11 NIV

Paul was so thankful for his friends in Thessalonica. They had given their lives to Jesus, and their newfound faith was flourishing. Paul had heard about how they grew in their love for one another and accomplished good things because of their faith.

Paul also heard reports about how they were being persecuted for following Christ. He heard that they were suffering hardships in their livelihood because of their faith. Paul's heart broke for their situation, but he also was inspired by their courage. So, he prayed that the Lord would bless them even in times of persecution.

Lord, please give me success in the things you have called me to do. Help me honor you in all circumstances.

Scripture Reading: 1 Timothy 1-3

Above Reproach

The goal of our instruction is love from a pure heart, from a good conscience, and from a sincere faith.

1 TIMOTHY 1:5 NASB

Paul spent much of his letter to Timothy encouraging the young pastor to be faithful in his teaching and conduct. He reminded Timothy that there were people who claimed to follow God but didn't follow his ways and taught improper things about him. These people ended up teaching meaningless customs that led people away from Jesus.

Men who want to have a positive impact in the lives and faith of others should live above reproach. Paul says that such men should be faithful to their wives, exercise self-control, live wisely, and have a good reputation. Paul teaches Timothy that men who wish to be leaders should enjoy hosting others, be controlled in their drinking and in their temper, and display gentle strength.

Lord, help me be above reproach today in everything I say and do.

Scripture Reading: 1 Timothy 4-6

Personal Reflection

Keep a close watch on yourself and on the teaching. Persist in this, for by so doing you will save both yourself and your hearers.

1 TIMOTHY 4:16 ESV

What we say impacts the opinions people form about us. A person who is truthful in word and deed is a person who wins the trust of others. Likewise, if we claim to be a committed Christian, our words and actions impact the opinions people form about God.

The Apostle Paul suggests to Timothy that he could bring down his whole ministry if he were to be false in his teachings or actions. If he spoke untruths, his teaching could hinder people from knowing God. If he acted hypocritically, his behavior could cause people to walk away from faith. Paul's letter is a reminder that our behavior can impact the faith of others. This is a responsibility that shouldn't be taken lightly.

Lord, help me represent you well today. May my words and actions point people to you.

Scripture Reading: 2 Timothy 1-4

Fan into Flame

I remind you to fan into flame the gift of God, which is in you through the laying on of my hands, for God gave us a spirit not of fear but of power and love and self-control.

2 TIMOTHY 1:6-7 NIV

When Timothy was a young man, his mother and grandmother led him to Jesus. The example of their faith nurtured a deep commitment to God in Timothy's life. When the Apostle Paul met Timothy, he sensed the young man had a powerful calling to serve God as a pastor. Paul knew that the Spirit of God would not make Timothy timid, but would give him power, love, and self-control. Paul urged him to let that spirit spread like wildfire.

When we chose to follow Jesus, we received a spirit of power! We don't have to be slaves to fear. We are overcomers, and we have victory over our struggles because Jesus has saved us. We have also received a spirit of love. We have everything we need to be kind and compassionate because God loved us first. Lastly, we have been given a spirit of self-control. We can stand strong against temptation because God has fully equipped us.

God, increase your power in me today. Fan into flame the calling you have for me.

Scripture Reading: Titus 1-3

Teach Truth

Teach the truth so that your teaching can't be criticized. Then those who oppose us will be ashamed and have nothing bad to say about us.

TITUS 2:8 NLT

If Titus faithfully taught the truth of Scripture, no one would be justified to criticize him. However, if Titus taught inaccurately, criticisms of his carelessness or deceptive intentions would be appropriate. We can't teach whatever we want about God and expect our path to be smooth.

We are called to represent Scripture accurately. Biblical truth is more important than persuasive arguments are flashy, emotional speeches. The good news is we don't have to come up with wise anecdotes or compelling stories on our own. We can simply read the Word and tell people what it says. As we genuinely teach the truth, people will be drawn to the Lord.

Lord, may I be fully trustworthy in my words and actions today. Help me teach your truth in all that I say and do.

Scripture Reading: Philemon 1

Pathway to Freedom

I pray that your partnership with us in the faith may be effective in deepening your understanding of every good thing we share for the sake of Christ.

Philemon 1:6 NIV

In the early days of Christianity, as faith in Jesus spread rapidly across the Roman Empire, many people turned from their old ways of life to follow Jesus. One such person was a man named Onesimus. Onesimus was an indentured servant to Philemon who had run away and left Philemon at a loss.

Now, changed by Christ and desiring reconciliation, Onesimus was returning home to Philemon. He carried a letter, written by Paul, that urged Philemon to accept the runaway. Paul argued that both men had a new status and now belonged to wide-ranging network of followers of Christ. Onesimus wasn't Philemon's slave any longer, and Philemon didn't need to be a slave to the old cultural systems anymore. Jesus changes social structures and creates pathways to freedom for all people.

Jesus, thank you for bringing reconciliation to the least likely of scenarios. Bring healing to my heart where needed.

Scripture Reading: Hebrews 1-3

Overcoming Temptation

Because he himself has suffered when tempted, he is able to help those who are being tempted.

HEBREWS 2:18 ESV

How could God ever truly understand what it is like to be a tempted man? Does he realize how easy it is to be distracted by alluring thoughts and images? Does he know how hard it is to ignore feelings of anger toward someone who has wronged us? The incredible truth is that he does understand!

Jesus is our advocate who understands everything we experience. He walked this earth, and he lived among us. He talked, ate, laughed, and sang. He slept, worked, cried, and hurt. He knew what it was like to make a friend, and he knew what felt like to be betrayed. He experienced hunger, weakness, and temptation, yet Jesus did not give in. He trusted in his Father, and he was strengthened by the Word.

God, give me the courage and ability of my Savior when I face temptation today.

Scripture Reading: Hebrews 4-6

Full Confidence

Let's approach the throne of grace with confidence, so that we may receive mercy and find grace for help at the time of our need.

HEBREWS 4:16 NASB

There is no reason to hesitate before God. There is no reason to approach him timidly or full of shame. Jesus died on the cross so that we could have confidence in our position before the Father. That was the whole point. God longs for us to see him rightly and approach him with the expectation that he will be merciful.

We all fall short of God's glory. None of us are good enough to stand before him. God is fully aware of our flaws and weaknesses, and he wants us to come to him anyway. He wants us to throw our burdens at his feet and accept his gift of salvation. He doesn't want us to be entangled by our sins when we could be experiencing the freedom and joy found in his presence.

Jesus, I run to you with joy in my heart and praise in my soul. You are my Savior and my Redeemer.

Scripture Reading: Hebrews 7-9

Free to Worship

Just think how much more the blood of Christ will purify our consciences from sinful deeds so that we can worship the living God. For by the power of the eternal Spirit, Christ offered himself to God as a perfect sacrifice for our sins.

HEBREWS 9:14 NLT

We can rejoice in our salvation today. As followers of Jesus, we have reason to celebrate. He has taken away our sins and invited us to live in freedom. He has given us his Spirit, and we have a multitude of reasons to praise him. His sacrifice has given us everything we need.

The blood of Jesus has saved you. The consequence of your sin was taken upon his shoulders as he was nailed to the cross. The death and separation that was yours has been left in the tomb. You have been given everlasting life and freedom. You are no longer a slave to sin and fear, for Christ's righteousness has become your own.

Lord, you are worthy of all my praise. Thank you for dying in my place. Thank you for the life you've given me.

Scripture Reading: Hebrews 10-13

Stand for God

Strengthen your feeble arms and weak knees. "Make level paths for your feet," so that the lame may not be disabled, but rather healed.

HEBREWS 12:12-13 NIV

There have been many people who have faithfully lived for God in this world. They are a great cloud of witnesses according to the writer of the book of Hebrews. We are encouraged by believers like Noah, Abraham, Moses, and David. Their lives provide us with a testimony as to how God empowers people to trust and follow him.

Someday your life will be added to that cloud of witnesses. Your testimony matters, and the way God moves in your life is impactful. Your skills, talents, and circumstances aren't as important as your willingness to humbly follow the Lord. He will strengthen you, help you where you are weak, and empower you to stand firmly. Cast off whatever is holding you back and fix your gaze on God.

God, give me courage to stand for you. May the testimony of my life encourage others.

Scripture Reading: James 1-3

True Religion

Religion that God our Father accepts as pure and faultless is this: to look after orphans and widows in their distress and to keep oneself from being polluted by the world.

JAMES 1:27 NIV

The book of James has been convicting people for nearly two thousand years. When we read that faith without works is dead, we come face to face with the realization that our beliefs must impact the way we live. Our actions reveal the condition of our faith in God. If we claim to be saved by God, our behavior should reflect his character and purposes.

God's standards are different from ours. His idea of doing the right thing is taking care of orphans and widows. We might be tempted to come up with a list of rules to follow, but God's ways are more about loving and serving than maintaining our perception of goodness. God lifts up those who are overlooked, and we should do the same. That is what it means to honor him with our lives.

Lord, may my faith be evident in the way I live. Show me opportunities to love and serve your people.

Scripture Reading: James 4-5

Practice of Devotion

Submit yourselves therefore to God. Resist the devil, and he will flee from you. Draw near to God, and he will draw near to you. Cleanse your hands, you sinners, and purify your hearts, you double-minded.

James 4:7-8 ESV

The goal of a daily devotions is to draw closer to God. We practice daily submission by reading the Word, meditating on God's ways, and spending time in his presence. Daily habits help us properly prioritize God in our lives. Consistently acknowledging who he is and what he's done provides us with strength and increases our faith.

Leaning on the Lord every day looks different for everyone. Some people prefer quiet times of meditation while others connect with the Lord through nature. Some people engage in songs of worship while others listen to Scripture on their drive to work. There are a multitude of ways to connect with God, but the most important thing is that we are strengthened by drawing near to him.

Heavenly Father, draw me closer to your heart. Equip me to face the day and help me honor you in all I do.

Scripture Reading: 1 Peter 1-3

Fully Equipped

Prepare your minds for action, keep sober in spirit, set your hope completely on the grace to be brought to you at the revelation of Jesus Christ.

1 PETER 1:13 NASB

As believers we walk through a hostile world. There is a constant battle for our hearts, souls, and minds. Peter warns us that our holiness will be tested. His words call us to action and urge us to be mindful of what is really going on. He doesn't want believers to be lulled into submission to anything or anyone other than God.

A battle might be raging, but we are not alone or unprepared. God has given us everything we need to be victorious. Through Christ, we are fully prepared for whatever comes our way. We have the armor of God and the fruit of the Spirit at the ready. We have the encouragement of other believers, and we have the power of Scripture. We can walk through unexpected trials with confidence because we know that God will give us grace to overcome.

Lord, help me mindful of the enemy's schemes. Thank you for equipping me for whatever comes my way.

Scripture Reading: 1 Peter 4-5

Because He Cares

Humble yourselves, therefore, under God's mighty hand, that he may lift you up in due time. Cast all your anxiety on him because he cares for you.

1 PETER 5:6-7 NIV

We can imagine casting our cares upon God like a fisherman casts a net out to sea. This isn't a feeble toss or a gentle placement. We don't need to line up our anxieties nicely or give them God perfectly wrapped. We don't need to justify, defend, or explain our fears. We can cast, hurl, and heave our cares at his feet. We can unceremoniously throw our frustrations with all the strength we have.

Why can we cast our anxieties in this way? Because he cares for us. He longs to provide for us. He wants his children to know his goodness and experience the freedom he offers. He doesn't want a superficial relationship with neat and tidy interactions. He wants us to approach him authentically with confidence that he can handle whatever is in our hearts and on our minds. Our willingness to cast our cares upon him is directly related to our confidence in his ability to care for us.

Lord, thank you that I don't need to carry my anxiety on my own. I give my burdens to you today!

Scripture Reading: 2 Peter 1-3

Eyewitness to Jesus

We ourselves heard that voice from heaven when we were with him on the holy mountain.

2 PETER 1:18 NLT

Peter was an eyewitness to Jesus' life. He was one of the men who hauled in the miraculous catch, and he saw healings in his own home. He watched Jesus give sight to the blind, freedom to the possessed, and hope for the marginalized. He was with Jesus when he commanded a storm and walked on the water.

Peter also saw Jesus glorified in the presence of Moses and Elijah. He physically saw Jesus transfigured, and he heard the Father express his pride and love for his Son. We are encouraged by his eyewitness account, and we take his words to heart because we know they are more than clever stories. We are blessed to have such a beautiful collection of testimonies within the Word.

Lord, thank you for the testimony of Peter. Thank you for your encouragement to stand firm in my faith.

Scripture Reading: 1 John 1-3

Wise Investments

Everything in the world—the lust of the flesh, the lust of the eyes, and the pride of life—comes not from the Father but from the world. The world and its desires pass away, but whoever does the will of God lives forever.

1 John 2:16-17 NIV

Life is filled with opportunities to compromise. There are plenty of shiny schemes that try to catch our attention and tempt us to change our standards. The world promises immediate satisfaction for seemingly small sacrifices. The problem is that these little sacrifices add up, and before we know it, we are on the wrong path altogether.

The Bible advises us to invest in things that will last. John warns us to refrain from loving the world and give our devotion to Jesus instead. He calls us to walk in the light and encourage each other to stay faithful. He reminds us that Christ's blood purifies us from sin and promises us eternal rewards that will never fade away.

God, give me strength to say no to my fleeting desires. Help me invest in what is eternal.

Scripture Reading: 1 John 4-5

That We Might Live

This is how God showed his love among us: He sent his one and only Son into the world that we might live through him.

1 JOHN 4:9 NIV

Understanding God's love for us provides the foundation of our faith. It doesn't matter how much wisdom we have or how well we understand Scripture if we don't have love. We are saved by God's love, and we cannot understand him without starting with that truth. This realization causes us to respond to God in love, be filled by the love of his Spirit, and overflow with his love toward others.

God's great act of love initiates our acts of love toward others. How could we not be changed by God's love for us? How could we not love others after coming to know how God loves us? It's a natural progression that cannot be mustered up by human effort. We don't need to strive to create love; we need to experience it from God and allow it to overflow to the people around us.

Lord, let my life be marked by your love. Destroy selfishness in me by overwhelming me with your love.

Scripture Reading: 2 John 1

How to Love

Love means doing what God has commanded us, and he has commanded us to love one another, just as you heard from the beginning.

2 John 1:6 NLT

Sometimes men are given a hard time for seeming emotionally callous. It's suggested that men lack empathy or thoughtfulness for those around them. Over the years men have been referred to as neanderthals or robots when it comes to sentiment and compassion. If we use the world's standards for masculinity, we will surely miss the mark.

It's important to look at how the Bible portrays men. John sees no issue with men expressing love. He sees no barrier keeping men from expressing care for others. We can assume that Christ embodied masculinity perfectly, and he was gentle, kind, and compassionate. He was tender, thoughtful, and patient. Biblical manhood is about more than power, might, and strength.

Lord, help me see the full picture of what it means to be a God honoring man. Help me develop well rounded character that pleases you.

Scripture Reading: 3 John 1

Leadership Failure

Beloved, do not imitate what is evil, but what is good. The one who does what is good is of God; the one who does what is evil has not seen God.

3 John 1:11 NASB

Twenty percent of the fifteen verses of this chapter is devoted to the disappointing story of Diotrephes. He was an influencer in the early church who wanted to seize unhealthy control more than he wanted to promote healthy community. Diotrephes stirred up contention and division, spreading lies and defaming those he saw as competitors to power. Jude wrote this letter to his friend Gaius to encourage him to be unwavering even as Diotrephes undercut the Church.

Seeing a leader fail can be disappointing and difficult. When a leader sins, causes harm, or betrays trust, their bad example can create ripples of dysfunction. Unfortunately, leadership failure can be especially harmful in church settings, because church leaders are supposed to represent all that is good about God.

Lord, help me be a man who practices integrity in leadership even if others don't. Help me represent you accurately.

Scripture Reading: Jude 1

His Glory

Now to him who is able to keep you from stumbling and to present you blameless before the presence of his glory with great joy, to the only God, our Savior, through Jesus Christ our Lord, be glory, majesty, dominion, and authority, before all time and now and forever. Amen.

JUDE 1:24-25 ESV

Today's Scripture is an excellent summary of the Christian life. If we apply these words to our daily lives, our time on earth will be deeply meaningful and blessed. This profound passage puts us in our rightful place and God in his. Every phrase is power packed with understanding of who God is and who we are.

All glory and power belong to God. All majesty, dominion, and authority are his. Those things are not ours. We do ourselves a disservice when we try to operate outside of God' s intended order. His strength is not ours to steal or strive for. He offers us everything we need with great love and mercy. It is only right that we approach him with reverence and thanksgiving. He protects us and draws us into his presence not because of our greatness but because of his.

Lord, thank you for upholding me by your loving power today. Be glorified by my life today.

Scripture Reading: Revelation 1-3

Ears to Listen

"Whoever has ears, let them hear what the Spirit says to the churches. To the one who is victorious, I will give the right to eat from the tree of life, which is in the paradise of God."

Revelation 2:7 NIV

In these seven letters, Jesus speaks honestly to seven church communities that represent God's people. These letters were significant to those networks when Revelation was written, but they also contain long-term implications for everyone who has followed Jesus over the last two-thousand years.

Through these letters Jesus offers us wisdom for a variety of circumstances we might find ourselves in. He encourages those who suffer because of their faith. He challenges those who have become stagnant in their faith, and he warns those who have compromised in their faith. The overarching call to all believers is to listen to the Word of God and respond in obedience to his commands.

Jesus, give me grace to uphold an unwavering commitment to you. Help me respond every time you speak to me.

Scripture Reading: Revelation 4-6

He Is Worthy

One of the twenty-four elders said to me, "Stop weeping! Look, the Lion of the tribe of Judah, the heir to David's throne, has won the victory. He is worthy to open the scroll and its seven seals."

REVELATION 5:5 NLT

The world is groaning under the weight of sin and decay. Nations war against one another, diseases spread suffering and death, and hostility splits families and neighbors apart. No one can offer a solution for the world's problems. No one can initiate the rescue. All of our best intentions and plans will fail because no one is worthy to carry the burdens of humanity.

Jesus is the exception. He is fully God and fully man, and he is the one we look to for help. He is the Lion of the tribe of Judah. He is the Lamb of God who takes away the sin of the world. He is the solution to every problem, and the anecdote to our deepest suffering. He is worthy of the throne, and his sacrifice is the reason we are not doomed. He will be exalted in the end, and those of us who follow him will be lifted up as well.

Jesus, you alone are worthy of all glory, honor, and power. Take my life and make it yours.

Scripture Reading: Revelation 7-9

Beautiful Savior

They cried out in a loud voice:
"Salvation belongs to our God,
who is seated on the throne,
and to the Lamb!"

REVELATION 7:10 CSB

There is a powerful truth being proclaimed in the imagery of John's Revelation. He describes a scene where multitudes of people from every nation, tribe, and language stand before a throne of the Lamb. The people were wearing white robes and waved palm branches in their hands. Then they cried out, "Salvation belongs to our God, who is seated on the throne, and to the Lamb!"

Imagine the beautiful chorus being offered to Jesus. Imagine the endless song of gratitude and praise being lifted up toward his throne. Perhaps the most striking detail of today's passage is that the crowd worships him, and he responds by wiping away their tears. Jesus is the Shepherd to the multitudes. His response to our worship is to gather us, heal us, and take away our suffering forever. What a beautiful and worthy Savior!

Jesus, you are so worthy of all my praise! Thank you for being so merciful and gracious.

Scripture Reading: Revelation 10-12

Jesus Will Reign

Then the seventh angel blew his trumpet, and there were loud voices in heaven, saying, "The kingdom of the world has become the kingdom of our Lord and of his Christ, and he shall reign forever and ever."

REVELATION 11:15 ESV

Jesus will reign at the end of days. He is the King of Kings and Lord of Lords. When we feel overwhelmed by tragedies and chaos, we can lean upon his sovereignty. When we feel anxious about trouble and hostility, we can remember that we know the end of the story. Our Savior will rule and reign forever. God's kingdom will be established for all eternity.

Scripture promises us that Jesus has overcome the world. We can take heart because we know his promises are trustworthy. We can look at the unfolding of world events without stress or anxiety. We can find peace in knowing that he will bring all things under his authority. We might not know exactly how everything will play out, but we do know that God's plans will not fail.

Lord, forgive me for being short-sighted and overwhelmed by the troubles of today. Thank you for the reminder that you will reign over all things.

Scripture Reading: Revelation 13-15

The Song of Moses

They were singing the song of Moses, the servant of God,
and the song of the Lamb:
"Great and marvelous are your works,
O Lord God, the Almighty.
Just and true are your ways,
O King of the nations."
REVELATION 15:3 NLT

In the book of Exodus, Moses wrote a song of praise to God for rescuing the Israelites from slavery. "With your unfailing love you lead the people you have redeemed. In your might, you guide them to your sacred home," sang Moses. In a crescendo he praised, "The Lord will reign forever and ever!"

At the end of the Bible, John envisioned seven powerful angels overlooking a multitude of people who had been rescued by the Lamb of God. The angels held harps and launched into a song that combined the words of Moses with a new song of praise for the Lamb. The story of the Bible is cohesive. God has woven the details together since the early pages of Genesis until the end of time. His story is infinite, and his plans will be perfectly executed.

Lord, thank you for the cohesive and beautiful story of salvation.

Scripture Reading: Revelation 16-18

A Good Thief

"Look, I come like a thief! Blessed is the one who stays awake and remains clothed, so as not to go naked and be shamefully exposed."

REVELATION 16:15 NIV

The sixteenth chapter of Revelation describes the wrath of God being poured out upon demonic forces in a great battle. There is one verse that stands in stark contrast to all the others. There is an unexpected moment of calm like an eye in the middle of a storm. There is a brief but significant note of reprieve between scenes of death, destruction, horrors, and hailstorms. There is hope in the middle of seemingly hopeless circumstances.

We are promised deliverance by Jesus. He says that he will steal away those who seek him. He will rescue us from judgment. With stealth and skillfulness, he will break into the battle to lead those who are ready for freedom. As the world descends into destruction, Jesus will seek and find those who call upon his name. He will calmly walk into the storm and rescue his people.

Jesus, keep my focus sharp and undistracted. Help me stay faithful until the end. I trust you with my life and salvation.

Scripture Reading: Revelation 19-20

Only God

Then I fell down at his feet to worship him, but he said, "No, don't worship me. I am a servant of God, just like you and your brothers and sisters who testify about their faith in Jesus. Worship only God. For the essence of prophecy is to give a clear witness for Jesus."

REVELATION 19:10 NLT

John, the one who received this great revelation, recounted this moment when he fell to his knees to worship an angel. He was caught off guard by the angel's impressive radiance, and he surrendered himself in adoration. The angel quickly corrected John. He warned John not to worship him as he was just a servant of God.

We are meant to worship God alone. This has been a key theme throughout the entire Bible. From Genesis to Revelation, we are reminded that man is intended to give our worship to the one true God. Anything else that solicits our attention is not worth our time or energy. It's our responsibility to be mindful of our affections and to ensure that we are devoted to the Lord above all else.

God, don't let anyone take your place in my heart. Help me keep my eyes on you.

Scripture Reading: Revelation 21-22

Heart's Cry

He who testifies to these things says, "Surely I am coming soon." Amen. Come, Lord Jesus!

REVELATION 22:20 ESV

As we reach the end of the year, there is no better prayer to echo than the one found at the end of the Scriptures. "Come, Lord Jesus!" The cry of our hearts is for all things to be restored by Jesus. He will return in glory and banish evil. He will rid the world of pain and usher in eternal peace. He will quench every thirst with everlasting life.

It is easier to remain steady when Christ's return is the earnest cry of your heart. Let his promises give you strength in the midst of trials and hope in the midst of suffering. Look toward that day of perfection with great anticipation and delight. Remember that your devotion to God will not be without reward. The best is yet to come!

Come, Lord Jesus!